000 things you should know about

rocks & minerals

000 things you should know about

rocks & minerals

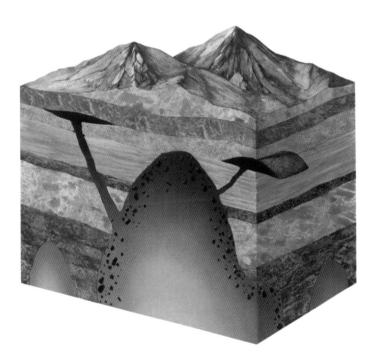

Chris and Helen Pellant

Miles Kelly
PUBLISHING

This material was first published as hardback in 2005

This edition published in 2006 by Miles Kelly Publishing Ltd
Bardfield Centre, Great Bardfield, Essex, CM7 4SL

2 4 6 8 10 9 7 5 3 1

Editorial Director: Belinda Gallagher
Art Director: Jo Brewer
Editor: Amanda Askew
Editorial Assistant: Bethanie Bourne
Volume Designer: Ian Paulyn
Additional Design: Candice Bekir
Picture Researcher: Liberty Newton
Reprographics: Anthony Cambray, Mike Coupe,
Stephan Davis, Ian Paulyn

British Library Cataloguing-in-Publication Data
A catalogue record for this book is available from the British Library

ISBN 1-84236-689-0

Printed in China

info@mileskelly.net
www.mileskelly.net

All artworks from the MKP Archives

All photographs from:
Castrol, CMCD, Corbis, Corel, DigitalSTOCK, digitalvision, Flat Earth,
Hemera, ILN, John Foxx, PhotoAlto, PhotoDisc, PhotoEssentials,
PhotoPro, Stockbyte
(Pages 7, 16, 17, 18, 20, 21, 28, 32, 34, 36, 37, 43, 44, 48, 55, 55, 57, 61)

All other photographs courtesy of
Chris and Helen Pellant

CONTENTS

What is a rock?

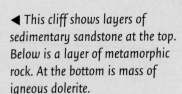

● **A rock** is an aggregate (mixture) of minerals. It may be made of sandstone or mudstone, fossil or fossil debris (limestone), or mineral crystals stuck together (igneous and metamorphic rocks).

● **Scientists classify rocks** into three main groups – igneous, sedimentary and metamorphic.

● **Rocks started forming** as soon as the molten (liquid) Earth began to cool 4000 million years ago.

● **The first rocks** were igneous. These formed from liquid magma underground, or lava on the surface.

● **Rocks form** in a cycle. Igneous rocks are weathered and eroded, and formed into sedimentary rocks. These may be altered by metamorphism (the effect of heat or pressure) and, if they are buried deep in the Earth's crust, they melt and become igneous rocks again.

● **The age of rocks** is worked out by studying fossils they contain or the breakdown of radioactive elements in them. This is called radiometric dating.

◀ This cliff shows layers of sedimentary sandstone at the top. Below is a layer of metamorphic rock. At the bottom is mass of igneous dolerite.

● **As soon as the Earth's atmosphere** began to develop 2000 million years ago, erosion and weathering began to break down igneous rocks to sediments.

● **Metamorphic rocks occur** when rocks change due to heat from magma or lava, or by pressure and heat underground.

● **Rocks are formed** all the time. Mud and sand on the beach or a riverbed may become a sedimentary rock.

> ★ STAR FACT ★
> The oldest rocks to be radiometrically dated are over 3900 million years old.

What are igneous rocks?

● **Geologists sometimes call igneous rocks** primary rocks because they form from molten material that originates deep in the Earth's crust.

● **Igneous rocks can be distinguished** from other rocks because they are made of a mosaic of mineral crystals, usually without layers.

● **The crystals in igneous rocks** are usually welded together.

● **Igneous rocks occur** in many different structures, both underground (intrusive) and on the surface (extrusive).

● **Intrusive igneous rocks form** underground in large masses called batholiths, and relatively small intrusions, for example, sills and dykes.

● **Extrusive igneous rocks build** volcanoes. These may have large rocky craters or be mountains of ash and dust.

● **Igneous rocks are the best** for radiometric dating as the crystals in them formed at a definite time in the past. These crystals may not have altered since formation, so an accurate date can often be obtained. Radiometric dating is most accurate if the rocks are fresh and unweathered.

● **Basalt is a volcanic igneous rock** that makes up more of the Earth's crust than any other rock. It covers the vast ocean basins.

● **Granite, an igneous rock** that forms underground, makes up much of the Earth's crust.

● **Some igneous rocks,** such as granite, are hard and durable and quarried for use in road surfaces.

◀ Crater Lake in Oregon, USA, is the remains of a collapsed volcano called a caldera. The small cone forms Wizard Island.

How igneous rocks vary

▶ Lava can erupt in a violent, frothy mass, containing a lot of gas. When it cools, it is full of gas-bubble holes.

● **Igneous rocks differ from each other** in two main ways – what they are made of and the size of their crystals.

● **The composition of an igneous rock** is not usually complex, and consists of very few minerals.

● **One main group of igneous rocks**, which geologists call felsic (acid) rocks, is made largely of three easily identified minerals – quartz, feldspar and mica.

● **Acid rocks are usually** pale-coloured and light.

● **Another important group** is made of feldspar, olivine and pyroxene, with only a small amount of quartz. These are called mafic (basic) rocks.

● **Basic rocks are generally** dark-coloured and heavier than you would expect when picked up.

● **If an igneous rock solidifies** as magma cools underground, its crystals are often large enough to see with the naked eye. Geologists call these rocks coarse-grained.

● **Igneous rocks that solidify** as lava cools on the Earth's surface have tiny mineral crystals. A microscope may be needed to see them. These rocks are fine-grained.

● **Sometimes magma or lava** cools in two stages – one deep underground and the other on, or near, the surface. If this happens, the rock will contain both large and small crystals.

● **Volcanic rocks** include a range of fragments blown to bits by an eruption. Examples are dust, ash and pumice.

Granite

▶ This granite on the Isle of Mull, Scotland, has been weathered along its vertical joints. The pink colour results from feldspar in the rock.

● **Granite** is one of the best-known igneous rocks due to its colourful, crystalline appearance.

● **It is a coarse-grained igneous rock** with crystals that are easily seen by the naked eye. They are generally more than 5 mm across. Granite also contains white or pink crystals of feldspar and black or silvery white mica.

● **Other minerals found in granite**, which do not affect its classification, are called accessory minerals. These include pyrite, tourmaline and apatite.

● **Granite contains a large amount** of quartz. This common mineral is off-white or grey, greasy-looking and very hard.

● **Granite forms deep in the Earth's crust** in large chambers of molten magma called batholiths. The magma cools slowly, often taking millions of years, which enables the crystals to grow to a large size.

● **For granite to be exposed at the surface**, thousands of metres of rock have to be weathered and eroded.

● **Rocks may also be pushed up** by mountain-building processes before granite is exposed at the surface.

● **Granite is not as durable** as we think. It weathers in humid climates, decomposing to sand and clay.

● **In the area around a mass of granite**, there is a region of metamorphism where heat from the magma has changed the original rocks.

● **In the area near a granite batholith** it may be possible to mine for minerals such as tin, lead and zinc.

Batholiths

- **A batholith is a very large mass** of igneous rock that was originally magma.

- **Most batholiths are formed** deep in mountain chains and may be tens of kilometres in diameter.

- **In Britain, a batholith exists** under much of Cornwall and reaches out under the sea to the Scilly Isles. This covers an area of 65 km by 40 km. Many batholiths are larger than this.

- **Before the giant mass of magma** in the batholith was intruded (forced in), there was other rock in that part of the Earth's crust. Geologists have puzzled over what happened to the original rock. It is believed that some of it was melted and incorporated into the magma.

- **Granite magma itself** may be the result of the melting of other rock at great depth.

▼ A batholith is a mass of magma formed deep below a mountain range. Small offshoots of magma may rise from it higher into the Earth's crust. Lumps of rock called xenoliths may be present in the batholith.

- **Sills and dykes** may stretch upwards from batholiths.

- **Most batholiths are made** of granite. Some contain other coarse-grained igneous rocks, such as syenite and gabbro.

- **Even when the rock in a batholith** has been crystalline for millions of years, heat will still rise through it from a great depth. This heat may be trapped if clay and other rock have formed later.

- **Scientists have discovered** that this heat could be used to produce electricity in a safe, clean way.

Batholith

Xenolith

Gabbro

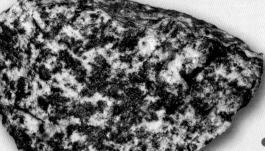

● **Gabbro forms** as large masses of magma cool, as granite does, but it is made of different minerals. As it cools slowly, it has large, easily visible crystals.

● **Rather than occurring in batholiths**, gabbro is commonly found in thick sheets of igneous rock.

● **Feldspar and pyroxene are the two main minerals** in gabbro, but it also has a small amount of quartz – less than 10 percent.

● **Feldspar is a pale mineral**, often occurring in thin crystals in gabbro, while pyroxene is almost black, giving the rock its speckled appearance.

● **Compared with granite**, gabbro is a very dark-coloured rock, and is also noticeably heavier.

◄ *Gabbro is a dark igneous rock. It is made of quite large crystals and has a speckled appearance.*

● **It is heavier because it contains** a large amount of pyroxene, which is a dense mineral.

● **A mineral called olivine** is sometimes found in gabbro. This is a green or brownish mineral, rich in iron and magnesium, which crystallizes at very high temperatures.

● **Gabbro mainly forms in the Earth's crust** beneath the basalts of the ocean floors but can also occur on continents. Granite typically occurs in a continental setting.

● **Some famous masses of gabbro** are at Bushveldt in South Africa and Stillwater, Montana, USA.

● **In Britain**, the Cuillin Hills on the Isle of Skye in western Scotland are largely made of gabbro, which weathers into jagged peaks.

Pegmatite

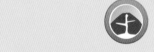

● **Pegmatite is an igneous rock** formed underground and made up of large crystals. These may be over 3 cm long. In some pegmatite, giant crystals over one metre long have been found.

● **For such large crystals to form**, the magma must cool slowly, allowing the crystals a long time to develop.

● **Pegmatite occurs in sheets** and other structures, often around the margins of large-scale intrusions.

● **Sills and dykes of pegmatite** also occur in many areas of very old gneiss.

● **Pegmatite often** has a similar composition to granite, containing mainly feldspar, mica and quartz. Gabbro and syenite pegmatites are not uncommon.

◄ *This pegmatite is full of pink feldspar crystals. It has cut into dark metamorphic rock.*

● **Pegmatite generally crystallizes** from magma or other high-temperature fluids, which are rich in rare elements such as niobium and tungsten.

● **Extra minerals often found in pegmatites** are tourmaline, topaz, fluorite, apatite and cassiterite.

● **Radioactive elements**, such as autunite and torbernite, also occur in pegmatite.

● **Some pegmatites have an appearance** called graphic texture. This looks like ancient writing and is created by quartz and feldspar crystals merging.

● **A crystal of the mineral beryl** nearly 6 m long, and a spodumene crystal over 15 m long, were found in a pegmatite in South Dakota, USA.

Xenolith

- **The word 'xenolith'** comes from the Greek *xenos*, which means 'stranger' and lithos, meaning 'stone'.

- **Xenoliths are found** around the margins of many igneous intrusions, where magma has melted and forced its way into other rocks. They may also be found in lava.

- **Xenoliths are broken off rocks** that have been engulfed by igneous rock, so are strangers in a new location.

- **They often appear** as dark, rounded or irregular rocks set in granite or other igneous rock.

- **At the edge of the igneous intrusion**, a xenolith will not have been overheated by magma and keeps many original features.

- **Xenoliths found some metres** into the igneous rock will have been altered considerably.

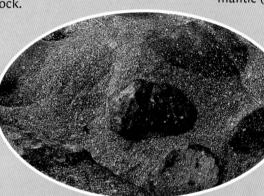

- **Xenoliths help geologists** work out the types of rock magma passed through as it was being intruded or erupted.

- **In some places** blocks of the lowest crustal rocks have been brought to the surface by magma. These let geologists study rocks rarely seen at the surface.

- **In the diamond-bearing rocks around Kimberly**, South Africa, xenoliths that may be derived from the Earth's mantle (the region beneath the crust) are found.

- **Large amounts of xenolith rock** caught up in magma may react with it and change its composition.

◀ Large, dark xenoliths can be easily seen in this eroded mass of igneous diorite. They were surrounded by molten magma and partly changed by its heat.

Syenite

- **Syenite is an intrusive igneous rock** that has formed by the cooling of magma deep in the Earth's crust.

- **Due to the slow cooling** associated with the high temperatures at great depth, syenite has large crystals and is a coarse-grained rock.

- **Syenite may look** rather like granite, but by studying the minerals it contains, differences can be seen.

- **Syenite will usually appear darker-coloured** than granite, but not as dark as gabbro. Some syenites may be pink or grey, or tinged with violet.

- **One well-known type of syenite** is called larvikite. It is from Norway and is often cut into slabs and polished to make a pearly blue-green stone. This has been used as a facing stone on many buildings throughout the UK.

- **As well as occurring in large intrusions**, syenite is found in sills and dykes. These rocks have smaller crystals.

- **Many syenites** have big crystals set in a finer mass. This gives an attractive appearance called a porphyritic texture.

▶ Syenite has large crystals because it formed as magma cooled slowly. The pale crystals are feldspar and the darker patches are made of mica, pyroxene and hornblende.

- **As well as feldspar and quartz**, syenite can contain hornblende, pyroxene and the dark mica biotite. This composition contains features of both granite and gabbro.

- **Microsyenite** is an igneous rock with the composition of syenite but contains smaller crystals.

- **Rhomb porphyry** is a type of microsyenite found commonly in Norway. Pebbles of it, which have been carried by ice sheets across the North Sea area, are often found on the east coast of England.

Dykes and sills

● **Dykes and sills** are called minor igneous intrusions because they are moderate to small in size.

● **Both intrusions** are sheets of igneous rock and are commonly made of rocks, such as dolerite, that have cooled quite quickly and are fine-grained.

● **They are usually measured in metres**, being anything from one or two metres in thickness to a few hundred.

● **A dyke is very often** a vertical sheet of dark rock cutting across existing strata (layers). Geologists call this a discordant intrusion.

● **The magma forming** the dyke will have risen into a fracture in the overlying rocks.

● **Dykes are often found in great numbers**, or swarms. One such swarm occurs in the Inner Hebrides across southern Scotland and stretches into the north of England.

● **A sill, in contrast, follows** the rock structures in the area where it is intruded. This is called a concordant intrusion. In sedimentary rocks, they are generally intruded along bedding planes.

● **As they are small structures** giving out little heat, there is usually only a small metamorphic effect on neighbouring rocks.

● **Like many lava flows**, sills may form vertical columns of rock that results from the way the magma has cooled. This is known as columnar jointing.

> ★ **STAR FACT** ★
> On the Isle of Arran, Scotland, 525 dykes occur within a distance of 24 km. These have stretched the Earth's crust by 7 percent.

▼ *Dykes and sills are both small igneous intrusions. Dykes cut across the strata and sills follow the existing layers of rock.*

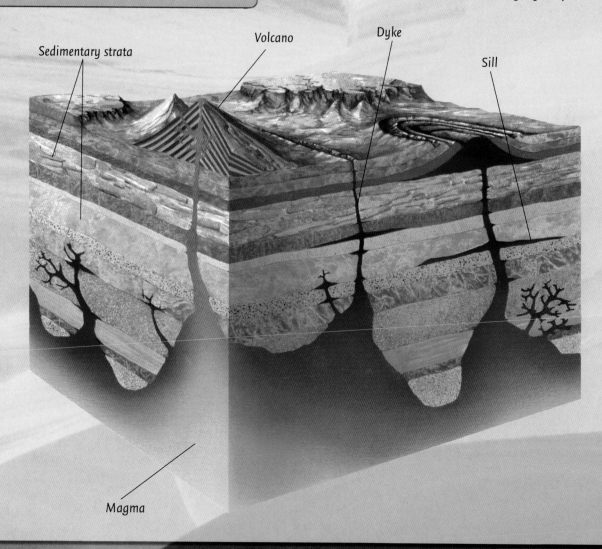

Sedimentary strata

Volcano

Dyke

Sill

Magma

Dolerite

- **Dolerite** is a dark igneous rock, often with an overall speckled appearance.

- **The speckled surface** results from the minerals it contains. These are light-coloured feldspar and black pyroxene. There is also a small amount of grey quartz. This is the same composition as gabbro and basalt.

- **Dolerite may contain** the green or brownish mineral called olivine.

- **It is possible to see its crystals** with the naked eye, but to study them in detail a strong lens is needed. Geologists call this type of rock medium-grained.

- **Dolerite commonly occurs** in small igneous intrusions, such as sills and dykes, where magma has cooled much more rapidly than in a batholith.

◀ As dolerite forms from magma that has cooled quickly, its crystals are not easy to see. A lens is needed to see the crystals in detail.

- **Rounded vertical masses of dolerite** may be the necks of old volcanoes. These remain after the lava and ash of the volcano have been eroded.

- **Dolerite-forming magma originates** very low in the Earth's crust or in the upper mantle. The rock is generally associated with thin oceanic crust rather than areas of thick continental crust.

- **Dolerite is a dense**, heavy rock mainly because it contains minerals that are rich in iron.

- **American geologists use the term** diabase for this type of rock.

- **Dolerite is a hard, durable rock**. It is extensively quarried for road stone, railway ballast and other uses.

Serpentinite

- **Serpentinite is thought** to be formed by the chemical alteration of other igneous rocks.

- **It often has shades of green** and red, which make veins in the rock.

- **As it is easily cut**, shaped and polished, serpentinite is often used ornamentally.

- **Serpentinite is made largely** of 'serpentine' minerals. These include chrysotile and antigorite, which are silicate minerals with a soapy feel and fibrous structure.

- **Chrysotile** is a source of asbestos, once used for its insulating properties.

- **Serpentinites contain virtually no quartz**, but can contain a number of silicate minerals, such as garnet, mica, hornblende and pyroxene.

- **It is generally believed** that serpentinites were originally dense, heavy rocks related to the lowest parts of the Earth's crust. These were rich in minerals such as olivine, and have been altered by the addition of water.

- **Some examples** give little indication of the original rock as the serpentinization is so extreme.

- **Serpentinites are found** in many areas, including New Zealand, New South Wales, Australia, and Montana, USA, and Cornwall, Anglesey and Shetland, UK.

- **Serpentine minerals are also found** in a group of meteorites called carbonaceous chondrites.

◀ The Lizard Peninsula, Cornwall, UK, where serpentinite occurs.

Volcanoes

● **A volcano is an opening** in the Earth's crust through which lava escapes.

● **Depending on the type of lava** and other volcanic materials, the volcano may be a low, gently sloping structure or a steep, cone-shaped mountain.

● **Some volcanoes have** a single opening. These are called central volcanoes. Others have a number of vents and are called fissure volcanoes.

● **Volcanoes from which basalt lava erupts** are not as violent as those that produce rhyolite and andesite lavas. Basaltic lava has a higher temperature and a less sticky silica than rhyolite and andesite lavas. This means that it flows easily away from the vent.

● **The Hawaiian, or shield, volcanoes** are made of basalt. They have large craters and low domes that spread many tens of kilometres. The base of Mauna Loa in Hawaii is 112 km in diameter.

● **Strombolian volcanoes**, named after the island of Stromboli to the north of Sicily, are classic cone shapes. Eruptions can be violent. As well as lava, there are layers of ash and dust.

● **Vesuvian volcanoes**, named after Mount Vesuvius in Italy, erupt only once every ten or more years. The lava is sticky and plugs the vent, causing violent eruptions.

● **Pelean volcanoes**, named after Mount Pelee in Martinique, are amongst the most violent. These erupt sticky, silica-rich lava, which often solidifies in the volcano. A great pressure then builds up as more lava tries to get through, and much of the volcano is blown apart by the eruption.

● **Volcanoes can be very destructive**. In 1883, Krakatoa in Java erupted, sending a huge dust cloud around the Earth's atmosphere. This affected the climate for three years. Over 36,000 people died as a result of the eruption.

▶ Lava, ash, rock fragments and gas are all erupted from this volcano. The cone is built up of layers of lava and ash.

★ **STAR FACT** ★
Mauna Loa in Hawaii is the world's largest active volcano. From the seabed it is over 9144 m high.

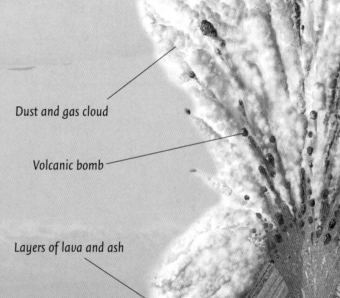

Dust and gas cloud

Volcanic bomb

Layers of lava and ash

Volcanic pipe

Where volcanoes occur

- **The distribution of volcanoes** is closely linked to lines of weakness in the Earth's crust and its varying thickness.

- **In ocean areas**, the crust is less than 10 km thick, but below the continents it may be 60 km thick. Lava can escape more easily to the surface where the crust is thin.

- **The Earth's crust** and the uppermost part of the underlying layer, the mantle, make up the lithosphere. This is divided into a number of plates.

- **The lithospheric plates are internally solid** but constantly move. Some collide, others move away from each other. It is along these plate boundaries that volcanic activity is concentrated.

- **The 'Ring of Fire' around the Pacific Ocean** has been studied for many years as many of the world's volcanoes are located in this region. The Pacific Ocean floor is the largest of Earth's plates and around its edges are weaknesses where erupting basaltic lavas can well up to the surface.

- **The volcanoes in Southeast Asia**, Japan, South and North America are all part of the Ring of Fire.

- **In the Atlantic**, the situation is different. Two major plates make up this ocean basin, which are moving away from each other. The Mid-Atlantic Ridge, which is mainly below sea level, is a line of active volcanoes.

- **In Iceland**, the Mid-Atlantic Ridge reaches above sea level. This island is made almost entirely of volcanic rock.

- **There are other regions** where eruptions are caused by plates moving apart from each other. The African Rift Valley is one place where this process is beginning – volcanoes such as Kilimanjaro occur.

- **The Hawaiian volcanoes** are in the centre of the Pacific plate, forming a chain of islands. They lie above a plume of hot material rising from the base of the crust.

▼ On the deep ocean bed where slabs of the Earth's crust move apart, lava erupts to form a range of underwater volcanic mountains.

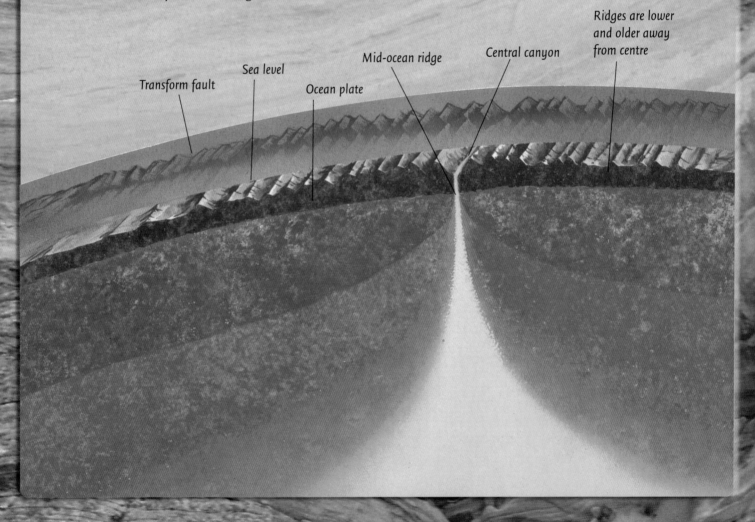

Transform fault

Sea level

Ocean plate

Mid-ocean ridge

Central canyon

Ridges are lower and older away from centre

Basalt

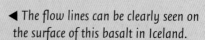

- **Basalt** makes up more of the Earth's crust than any other rock.

- **Volcanic basalt** often erupts non-violently and can flow great distances.

- **It is a dark-coloured rock** and its crystals can rarely be seen on its surface without a microscope. Basalt is what geologists call a fine-grained rock.

- **The composition of basalt** is the same as that of gabbro and dolerite. It contains crystals of feldspar, pyroxene and common olivine, and a little quartz.

- **When it erupts**, basalt lava contains gas. As the rock cools, gas-bubble hollows are left in the rock. These are called vesicles, and give the rock a rough texture.

- **Many minerals develop** in the vesicles, often after the rock has cooled.

◀ *The flow lines can be clearly seen on the surface of this basalt in Iceland.*

- **Basalt is a dense**, heavy rock. It contains iron-rich minerals that have been used to work out movements of the Earth's plates.

- **Basalt lava flows** often develop regular six-sided columns when cool. The Giant's Causeway in Northern Ireland is an example of this.

- **Basaltic rocks recovered from the Moon** contain similar minerals to those found on Earth.

★ STAR FACT ★
In the Deccan area of north-west India, basalt lava flows reach a thickness of nearly 2000 m and cover about 30 percent of the area of peninsular India.

Obsidian

▶ *Obsidian is formed from lava that cools so fast, it turns to glass. The white spots in this snowflake obsidian are where the glass has been altered.*

- **When lava erupts** onto the Earth's surface, it is suddenly in an environment 1000°C cooler than the one it was in underground.

- **This temperature change** causes the lava to freeze and solidify rapidly, with no visible crystals.

- **Obsidian is a rock** that is formed under these conditions, and it contains no real crystals.

- **Geologists have discovered** that obsidian is related to granite in composition and to another volcanic rock called rhyolite.

- **Pitchstone is a rock** that is rather like obsidian, but contains more crystalline material and its surface is more like pitch, or tar.

- **When broken**, obsidian has a very sharp, curved surface. This is called a conchoidal (shell-like) fracture.

- **Its sharp fracture has been exploited** by primitive people for making weapons and other implements, as it can be easily and accurately shaped.

- **Snowflake obsidian is an attractive rock** covered with small white patches. These occur where the volcanic glass has deteriorated. This rock is often cut and polished.

- **Obsidian is a well-known rock**, but is not very common. Hecla in Iceland and Obsidian Cliff in Yellowstone National Park, USA are famous locations.

★ STAR FACT ★
The most striking feature of obsidian is that it looks just like a piece of black glass.

Tuff and bombs

● **As well as lava**, volcanoes erupt broken rock, dust, ash and volcanic bombs.

● **Ash and dust** may be thrown high into the atmosphere. Much of this falls near the volcano.

● **When it has settled on the ground** and hardened into rock, this material is called tuff. It may have features of sedimentary rocks, such as layers or strata.

● **Ignimbrite is a type of tuff** in which the fragments are welded together. They are erupted from Peleean volcanoes.

● **When Mount Pelee on Martinique** erupted in 1902, an ignimbrite flow covered the town of St Pierre, 8 km away, in minutes. The 30,000 inhabitants were buried under welded tuff, which reached nearly 1000 °C.

● **In 1815 the volcano Tabora**, in Indonesia, erupted with such force that 30 cubic km of dust was blown into the atmosphere. The dust masked the Sun and caused 1816 to be called 'the year without summer'.

◀ *Volcanic bombs are lumps of molten lava flung high into the air by a violent eruption.*

● **Droplets and larger lumps of lava** flung into the air form volcanic bombs.

● **Breadcrust bombs** are chunks of lava around which a crust forms. Molten lava inside releases gas and the crust cracks, giving the appearance of a loaf of bread.

● **Bombs usually have** a vesicular texture, being riddled with gas-bubble cavities.

● **In Hawaii**, lava spray forced through small openings and blown into strands by the wind is called Pelee's hair. Pelee is a mythical lady who is said to live in the volcano.

Rock columns

● **There are famous igneous rock formations** where the rock is in almost perfect vertical columns. These include The Giant's Causeway (Antrim, Northern Ireland) and Waikato Dam, (North Island, New Zealand)

● **The columns may be** many tens of metres high and can be perfectly symmetrical and usually six-sided.

● **The igneous rock involved** is very often basalt, although dolerite, rhyolite and welded tuff may also form columns.

● **Columnar structures are seen best** in lava flows, but they also form less perfectly in sills.

● **Sills and lava flows** have vertical columns as they cool from the base and top. In a dyke, columns may develop horizontally as the rock cools from its vertical edges.

● **When a lake or pond dries out**, wet mud on its bed shrinks into a pattern of polygonal cracks. Igneous rocks behave like this but in a more regular way.

▶ *The Giant's Causeway in Northern Ireland is a mass of interlocking basalt columns.*

● **Such regular shapes** form in cooling rock due to contraction and an even loss of heat.

● **As a lava flow ceases to move**, it begins to cool and form solid igneous rock. The base cools regularly and contraction begins to occur. Cracks develop and columns grow upwards through the lava.

● **Columnar formations usually have** a more perfect lower part and a less regular shape towards the top.

● **A hexagonal shape allows the columns** to fit together perfectly, but there can be columns with three to eight sides.

Rock pillows

- **Rounded masses of lava** called pillow lavas are well-known in the geological record.

- **The ocean floors are made** of basalt lava with a covering of sediment. Fresh basalt lava is continually erupting along the mid-ocean ridges.

- **On the deep seabed**, the composition of basalt lava changes to form a rock called spilite.

- **The 'pillow' shape is caused** as a skin cools around each mass of lava. Inside this, molten lava keeps moving, giving a rounded shape.

- **The lava may contain gas** that enlarges the pillows and gives the rock special texture. Gas-bubble holes are left in the lava after the gas escapes. This is called vesicular texture.

◄ *These pillows were formed on the deep seabed over 500 million years ago.*

- **The vesicles in pillow lavas** usually occur in rings that follow the pillow shape. In other lavas, they are randomly situated.

- **On the deep seabed**, pillow lavas are found with other rocks. Often they occur with mudstones.

- **Pillow lava can also form** when basalt erupts into wet mud, or below an ice sheet.

- **The spaces between the pillows** may be filled with broken lava fragments or a rock called chert. This is a very hard, silica-rich material.

- **Pillow lava occurs** in many parts of the world including Britain, south-east Germany, Washington, USA and North Island, New Zealand.

Geothermal springs

- **In many areas** where volcanic activity takes place (or has recently occurred), there are hot springs, or geysers.

- **The word 'geyser'** comes from the Icelandic *geysir*, meaning a 'spouter'. In Iceland, there are a number of regions where heated underground water gushes to the surface.

- **Hot water from underground** is used in Iceland for central heating and heating greenhouses.

- **In many regions** – such as California, USA and Weiraki, New Zealand, projects have been established to try to generate electricity from underground steam.

- **An individual geyser consists of** a central pipe with branches leading from it at depth. Water heated volcanically underground becomes pressurized. As the mass of water boils, it bursts vertically through the central pipe and into the air.

- **A number of geysers** are very regular in their spouting, and they remain constant over many years.

- **On the surface**, a geyser is surrounded by a pool of silica-rich water at a temperature of about 85°C. Deposited in this and around its margins is a silica rock called geyserite.

- **A piece of wood taken from geyserite** surrounding Old Faithful geyser in Yellowstone National Park, USA, has been dated at 730 years old. This says how long the geyser has been spouting.

- **The geyserite deposited** around geysers at Rotorua, New Zealand, has built the famous pink and white terraces.

- **The Romans appreciated** the value of hot springs for bathing and laundry.

◄ *The Old Faithful geyser in Yellowstone National Park, USA, flings steam into the air every hour.*

Uses of igneous rocks

● **Due to their attractive crystalline surfaces**, igneous rocks, such as granite and porphyry, are cut and polished for use in buildings. These rocks are frequently found as facings in commercial buildings.

● **Many granites and related rocks** have large crystals of pink and white feldspar, which look attractive.

● **It is currently fashionable** to use 'so-called' granite for kitchen work surfaces. The dark-coloured igneous rocks used in this way are actually syenites, not granite.

● **The appearance of igneous rocks** is often copied and printed onto other material for use as flooring and surface coverings.

● **Larvikite** is a type of syenite. It is made of feldspar crystals, which have a silvery sheen.

● **Many igneous rocks** are also very durable. Rocks such as dolerite and basalt, are extensively quarried and then crushed to the required size or grade.

● **Road ballast is a major use** of crushed igneous rock. One kilometre of new road requires 10,000 tonnes.

● **Aggregate, often made from finely crushed igneous rock**, is used in concrete and cement. Over 2000 tonnes of aggregate may be required for a new office block.

● **As well as being physically strong**, igneous rocks are less susceptible to the effects of acid rain than other rocks.

● **Cemeteries use igneous rocks** in the form of polished gravestones.

◄ *Tower Bridge, spanning the Thames River in London, is partly clad with Cornish granite.*

What are sedimentary rocks?

● **Sedimentary rocks** are best recognized by their layers. These result from the way the sediment has been deposited.

● **These rocks are formed** in a variety of environments on the Earth's surface, and in many cases are easier to study than igneous rocks, which often form at great depths.

● **Many sedimentary rocks are made of particles** that have been eroded or weathered from pre-existing rocks. For this reason, they are often referred to as secondary rocks.

● **The particles are transported by rivers**, wind, glaciers and gravity. During this journey they are changed and may become smaller, more rounded and broken.

● **Eventually, the particles** are deposited. A river can only carry big pebbles as it flows swiftly.

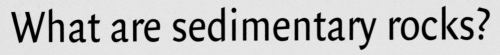

◄ *Like sand, sandstone may be any colour, but the most common colours are brown, yellow and white*

● **Most sedimentary rocks form** on the seabed. A river entering the sea slows down, depositing its load. The continental shelves have a great thickness of sediment, but much also reaches deeper parts of the oceans.

● **By looking at the features** of sedimentary rocks and comparing them to how modern sediments form, geologists work out what past environments were like.

● **Many sedimentary rocks** have economic significance. Coal was the power behind the Industrial Revolution and is still an important fuel for generating electricity.

● **Our knowledge of evolution** is based on fossil records. Fossils are preserved in sedimentary rocks.

● **Well-known sedimentary rocks** include sandstone, limestone, mudstone or shale.

Weathering

● **Rocks exposed on the Earth's surface** are broken down in many ways. Weathering causes rock decomposition without involving any movement, or transportation.

● **Weathering is the first** of many processes of denudation (wearing away). These processes result in an overall lowering of the land surface.

● **Many external agents are involved** in weathering, including temperature changes, rain, wind, bacteria, animals and plants.

● **Weathering produces the particles of rocks** and minerals, which are then transported and deposited as sedimentary rocks.

● **Mechanical weathering is mainly** the result of temperature changes. Water in cracks and joints in rocks expands when it freezes. This creates stresses, which cause rock disintegration. At the base of many mountain slopes and cliffs are scree slopes made of mechanically weathered fragments.

★ **STAR FACT** ★
Since the last ice age ended about 10,000 years ago, limestone pavements in North Yorkshire, UK, have weathered vertically by half a metre.

● **Temperature changes can cause** the different minerals in a rock to expand and contract at different rates. Stress produced in this way may lead to thin sheets of rock peeling off like the skin of an onion.

● **Chemical weathering affects** many rocks. Limestones are particularly vulnerable. Rainwater is a mild, natural carbonic acid, and with increased acid rain, it becomes more acidic.

● **Limestone itself is not soluble** in rainwater. Calcium carbonate, of which limestones are largely composed, reacts with acid rainwater and soluble calcium bicarbonate is produced.

● **Granite, often regarded as indestructible**, is far from it. The most common mineral in granite is feldspar, which is easily weathered by acid water, especially in tropical conditions. The feldspar rots to clay and the granite is reduced to an incoherent mass of quartz and mica sand.

▶ When rocks are heated and cooled in deserts, flakes break off to leave a rounded core.

◀ Tree roots grow into joints in many rocks. As the roots get larger, the rock is forced apart.

▲ In cold climates, water in cracks in the rock turns to ice, forcing the layers apart and fragments are broken off.

Erosion

- **Erosion is the breakdown of rocks** and wearing away of the land surface by processes that involve movement.

- **There are many different environments** in which erosion takes place, including rivers, glaciers and deserts.

- **River erosion occurs** mainly where rapid streams cut valleys through the land. Valley sides are eroded, as is the debris in the water.

- **River erosion can be seen** by the depth to which the Colorado River has cut its V-shaped canyons in Arizona, USA.

- **A glacier erodes** a deep, straight valley that has a U-shaped profile. Eroded rock is carried on and within the ice, and deposited when the ice melts.

▶ Arches National Park, USA. Sand-laden wind erodes rocks into amazing shapes.

- **As a glacier moves**, rocks frozen in the ice scrape at the bedrock, making marks called striations. Ice freezes into these and plucks rock fragments away as it moves.

- **At the coast**, waves containing sand and pebbles break against cliffs and scour rock pavements. Cliffs are further reduced by landsliding, often assisted by water running over the cliff face or seeping from rocks.

- **In deserts**, sand picked up by the wind blasts at any upstanding rock masses, concentrating at ground level. Rock pillars are sculpted this way.

- **Large rock fragments that are too heavy** to be picked up by the wind are eroded into three-sided 'dreikanter'.

- **Wind laden with fine sand** can strip the paint from vehicles within an hour.

How sedimentary rocks are formed

- **Weathering and erosion** provide particles from which sedimentary rocks are made.

- **Sediments may form rocks** with no alteration, by lithification. If physical or chemical changes occur in formation, the process is called diagenesis.

- **Most sediment is deposited** in the sea. Pore spaces fill with water. This must be removed to turn sediment to rock.

- **As sediment builds up**, weight and pressure affect lower layers. Water may be squeezed out, and the grains packed together, reducing pore space.

- **When sediment is first deposited in water**, it is mostly made up of gaps between the grains called pore spores. As the sediment is buried in the Earth's crust, the pore spores are reduced.

- **Sometimes, where weight is considerable**, sand grains weld together, removing pore spaces.

- **Many rocks stay porous** and may be a source of underground water, gas or oil.

- **Mineral-rich fluids seep into pore spaces** and form cements that bind individual particles in sedimentary rocks. A common cement is calcite. Quartz (silicon dioxide) is another cementing mineral. This chemically resistant cement is common in sandstones.

- **Limestones are largely made of calcite**, often derived from organic matter. Recrystallization may occur and the organic material dissolved and replaced by crystalline calcite.

- **Many sediments undergo colour changes** as they harden. Iron compounds seeping into pore spaces may colour sandstone red or yellow.

◀ These layers of sand and pebbles may one day become sandstone and breccia.

Environmental evidence

▲ *The sea leaves ripple marks on the sand as the tide goes out.*

● **Sedimentary rocks contain** evidence that geologists use to identify the environment in which the rock was originally deposited. This may be in the ocean, on a beach, or in a desert.

● **Each environment leaves clues** in the rock. Geologists study these to work out the depositional environment.

● **The size of the grains in rock** is important. On a beach, there are large pebbles, and out at sea, mud, silt and sand. Powerful currents carry large grains of sediment, and only fine mud can be taken into the deepest oceans.

● **On wet sand**, at low tide, the sea makes ripple patterns. Similar patterns are common on sandstones, suggesting they may have been deposited between tides.

● **A pattern of cracks occurs** as mud dries, for example, at the edge of a lake. Such cracks are found on many strata, suggesting the rocks were formed from lake mud.

● **Mud cracks can form** on tidal mudflats that dry up. Cracks may also form in shallow water (usually sea water).

● **As a river flows into the sea**, it may deposit a vast delta like that at the mouth of the Mississippi River in the USA.

● **There are different sedimentary rocks** in a delta. Across it run streams, which cut valleys in the mud. Channels in sandstones suggest they came from a delta.

● **If sandstone strata** are curved, the rock may have been formed in a desert – layers of sand in a dune are curved.

● **Fossils give clues** to where sediment was deposited. Some limestones contain fossil corals similar to those found in tropical seas today.

Sandstone

▶ *Small, rounded quartz grains can be seen in this sandstone specimen.*

● **Sandstone** is a common sedimentary rock. It is made of sand grains compressed together, or cemented by other minerals.

● **Sandstones can be created** in a variety of environments such as deserts, on the seabed, and in rivers and deltas.

● **Sand grains blown by the wind** tend to be rounded and slightly frosted in appearance. Those carried and deposited by water are usually more angular.

● **The main mineral in sandstone** is quartz. This mineral is chemically and physically resistant, so can withstand being transported some distance before being deposited.

● **Some sandstones contain** a relatively high proportion of feldspar. One example is a rock called arkose. Feldspar is easily weathered, so its presence in sandstone suggests that the sediment was deposited quickly.

● **Sandstones generally do not contain** as many fossils as other sedimentary rocks. However, those formed in the sea can contain mollusc shells, trilobites and ammonites. Delta sandstones contain plant fossils. Some of the best dinosaur fossils are from sandstones formed in riverbeds and on land.

● **Sandstone comes in different colours**. These are due to minerals, some of which cement the grains together.

● **Red and yellow sandstones contain** hematite and limonite around their grains.

● **Sandstones are used** for building as many can be cut into stones. Porous sandstones can hold water, oil or gas underground.

★ **STAR FACT** ★
On the bedding planes of certain sandstones, small glittery flakes can be seen. These are fragments of the mineral called mica.

Strata and folding

● **Many sedimentary rocks** are deposited in layers that geologists call strata. Each stratum represents the seabed or land surface at the time it was deposited.

● **Fossils are found** on strata. If deposition stops, plants and animals live on the surface. Their remains are covered and preserved when deposition resumes.

● **One principle of geology** is that as strata form, the oldest one is at the bottom and the youngest at the top.

● **If there is continuous deposition,** there will be no strata.

● **Strata can be linked** by their fossils. Ammonite fossils found in mudstone in Greenland, shale in Argentina and limestone in Italy prove these strata are the same age.

▶ *When rocks are highly compressed, tight folds can be formed.*

★ STAR FACT ★
Compression of the crust buckles strata into upfolds (anticlines) and downfolds (synclines).

● **Layers of sedimentary rock** are originally deposited horizontally. As the Earth's crust moves, they tilt and fold.

● **Younger strata** are horizontal, older ones are usually folded. However, the Torridonian sandstones in Scotland are over 900 million years old and have never folded.

● **Geologists measure features** of folded strata when they make geological maps. The greatest angle that can be measured down a sloping stratum is called the dip. This is shown on a map by an arrow pointing in the direction of the dip and a figure for the angle.

● **When the pressure is greater from one direction**, folding will be uneven and one side may tilt over above the other. This is a recumbent fold.

Conglomerate and breccia

● **Conglomerate is the name** geologists give to a sedimentary rock made of large, rounded fragments.

● **Pebbles and other fragments are held together** with a cement such as quartz, calcite or iron compounds.

● **The pebbles can be made of many materials.** Many conglomerates contain pebbles of quartz or quartzite.

● **Conglomerates are usually deposited** near to the area from which their fragments were eroded. Many conglomerates were deposited by rivers. This is because it takes a powerful river current to move such large particles.

● **Many conglomerates are beach deposits.** The fragments will be well-rounded because of being rolled backwards and forwards by the waves and tide.

● **Some conglomerates are the deposits** of flash floods in arid areas. Great masses of sand and pebbles lying on the land surface are easily washed along by powerful floods.

◀ *Breccia is made of large fragments of sedimentary deposits stuck together.*

● **Breccia is a rock** that is similar to a conglomerate. However its fragments are jagged and angular.

● **Breccia is deposited quickly**, sometimes without water transport, so its pebbles and other fragments do not get worn and rounded.

● **Many breccias are formed as scree** by the weathering of high mountain slopes.

● **Rock fragments are produced** when rocks move relatively to each other during faulting. The jumble of broken rock along the fault line is called fault breccia.

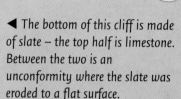

Time gaps

● **Sedimentary strata** are not deposited continuously. There have been considerable time gaps in deposition

● **A break in the geological record** is called an unconformity.

● **The unconformity is a rock surface.** Below it the rocks may be different – and much older.

● **Rocks below an unconformity** may be metamorphosed. Rocks above may be ordinary sedimentary rocks.

● **Geological time is recorded** by events in the rocks. An unconformity represents a break in this record.

● **In the far north-west of Scotland** is a classic unconformity. Its surface is rough land. Below are metamorphosed rocks dating back 2600 million years. Above the unconformity are stratified sandstones. These are 900 million years old. This means that 1700 million years of geological time are not recorded here.

◀ The bottom of this cliff is made of slate – the top half is limestone. Between the two is an unconformity where the slate was eroded to a flat surface.

● **Often geologists can only suggest** what might have happened during a time gap. Sometimes evidence from nearby, where more rocks have been preserved, can give clues.

● **An unconformity can represent** a time of erosion. This removes strata and a record of geological time.

● **Rocks may be folded or tilted** before erosion. This creates an angle between the older rocks and those above the unconformity. This is an angular unconformity.

● **When the rocks below and above** an unconformity are similar, fossils help to determine the age of the strata.

Manganese nodules

● **In the 1870s,** scientists on the research vessel *Challenger* found lumps of rock on the beds of the Atlantic and Pacific Oceans. As much as 35 percent of these were made up of manganese. Scientists called them manganese nodules.

● **The surface of each nodule** is rough and uneven, and when dry, is dark brown and dusty.

● **The nodules are complex inside.** They have an onion-like layering, built up around a grain of sediment or fossil fragment. Radiometric dating proves that it takes 40 million years for a 10 cm nodule to grow.

● **Manganese is one of many important metals** found in the nodules. They also contain copper, nickel and cobalt.

● **In 1962, a survey** of the Pacific Ocean bed found a vast deposit of manganese nodules at a depth of 5000 m.

● **Manganese nodules are also found** in the southern Atlantic Ocean, the Caribbean Sea and the Indian Ocean.

◀ Curved layers can be seen in this broken manganese nodule. This specimen was dredged from the Pacific Ocean.

● **Mining for the nodules** has been done out by the USA. The ship *Deepsea Miner* dredged the Pacific floor and recovered tonnes of nodules in the late 1970s.

● **There are problems mining** from the deep ocean floor. Even using computerized controls to position the ship, the venture has proved expensive.

● **About 5500 tonnes of nodules** would have to be recovered each day to make mining worthwhile. The impact of this on marine life would be huge.

● **Manganese nodules are a source** of metals. Cobalt and manganese are used in alloys for the oil refining industry.

Deep-sea sediments

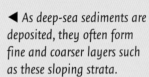

- **In the deepest part of the ocean**, sedimentary deposits accumulate. This is the abyssal part of the oceans.

- **Some sediment that turns to sedimentary rock** is deposited on the continental shelves.

- **The ocean does not have the force** to carry sand and pebbles so these are left near the shore. Only fine mud and clay travel to the ocean floor.

- **Icebergs have been known** to float far from their polar origins. Trapped in these huge blocks of ice is sediment, such as clay, sand or boulders.

- **Volcanic dust is often flung high** into the atmosphere. This dust can settle into the oceans and onto the seabed.

- **The ocean is filled with organisms** whose skeletons are made of calcite. These accumulate to form calcite-rich ooze, present to a depth of around 4000 m.

- **Marine organisms called diatoms** and radiolarians have skeletons made of silica. This material accumulates on the ocean floor to make silica ooze.

◄ As deep-sea sediments are deposited, they often form fine and coarser layers such as these sloping strata.

- **One unusual type of sediment** found in the deep ocean is made of repeated layers of sand and mud, deposited by rapidly flowing seabed (turbidity) currents, carrying sediment from the land.

- **In the geological record**, there are thousands of metres of dark, very fine sediment, called mudstone containing fossils of planktonic organisms.

- **Associated with dark-coloured shale**, geologists sometimes find repeated sand layers. These are proof that turbidity currents were at work in the past.

Limestone

- **Limestone is a sedimentary rock** that contains a high proportion of the mineral calcite (calcium carbonate).

- **Limestone is usually pale-coloured.** It can be dark due to a high percentage of mud and other eroded sediment.

- **Fossils are abundant** in most limestone such as coral limestone and shelly limestone, cemented together by calcite.

- **Most limestone deposits** are geologically young. Organisms with calcite shells, from which the rock is often made, did not evolve until Cambrian times.

- **Rainwater can mix with carbon dioxide** to form an acid strong enough to make limestone dissolve, sometimes forming underground caves in large rocks.

- **Oolitic limestone is made of small, rounded grains** of sediment. Concentric layers of calcite are formed around a small shell fragment or sand grain.

◄ Limestone can be packed with fossils such as the remains of water snails.

- **Dolostone** (dolomite) is a type of limestone. Dolomite is a double carbonate of calcium and magnesium.

- **Reef limestones contain fossils** of organisms that lived in the reef environment such as coral.

- **Some reefs may be composed** of a lime mud, secreted by various micro-organisms.

- **Limestone has many important economic uses** such as being an important building stone as it forms the basis of cement.

Chalk

▶ Chalk is made from
the remains of tiny
sea creatures.

● **Chalk** is a special
type of limestone. It is
a soft, white rock often
containing over
90 percent calcium
carbonate (calcite).

● **Chalk is a sedimentary
rock** that was deposited in the
sea, in regions where there was little seabed disturbance.

● **Most chalk occurs** in western Europe and in some parts
of North America. European chalk was deposited between
142 and 65 million years ago.

● **The famous white cliffs** along the south coast of
England, are composed of chalk.

● **One of the puzzles about chalk** is its great purity.
There is an almost complete lack of sand or mud and
other sediment carried from the land.

● **Much of the nearest land** was probably very low lying,
without hills and mountains. Because of this there would
have been very little erosion bringing mud or sand into
the sea.

● **Virtually all the calcite in chalk** is the remains of small
organisms. These include microscopic creatures called
coccoliths.

● **Large fossils are found in chalk.** These include
ammonites and other molluscs, brachiopods and
echinoids (sea urchins).

● **The layers of chalk are divided** into time zones using
ammonite fossils.

● **A variety of creatures lived in** and on the soft seabed.
Worms and sea urchins burrowed into the chalky mud.
Sponges and molluscs also lived on the seabed.

Flint

▶ When carefully chipped,
flint can be used to make tools
such as this pointed hand axe.

● **Flint is a hard, nodular
rock,** found in irregular layers
in chalk.

● **Flints can be seen** in chalk
cliffs as dark parallel bands
running among the white strata.

● **Like the common mineral quartz,** flint is composed of
silicon dioxide. Quartz usually forms hexagonal crystals
but the crystals making up flint are so small that a
powerful microscope is needed to see them.

● **The silica in flint is derived** from small sea creatures.
It is believed that concentrations of silica formed within
the chalk sediment and hardened into flint.

● **Large fossils are sometimes replaced by flint,** such
as the heart-shaped sea urchin called Micraster.

● **'False flints' are hollow inside.** Here the silica
formed around a sponge, that eventually disintegrated,
leaving a hollow. These false flints have a white powdery
interior made from the shells of single-celled
foraminiferans and ostracods (creatures related
to water fleas).

● **When flint is seen** on the surface of a chalk stratum,
the nodular lumps may occur in rings.

● **Flint is so hard** that it cannot be scratched with a knife
blade. It breaks easily into curved shapes with very
sharp edges.

● **The durability and sharpness of broken flint** has been
exploited in the past.

● **Early man used flints** to make hand axes from at least
2 million years ago. These were shaped by chipping flakes
of flint from around a core, using a hammer stone. Flint
has continued to be used in tools right up until the early
1800s when flintlocks were still being made.

Ice age rocks

● **The most recent ice age ended** in Britain and most of Europe and North America around 10,000 years ago. Evidence of this ice age is found in the landforms created by ice sheets and glaciers, and in their sedimentary rocks.

● **Glacial rocks are known** from much older times. There is evidence of an ice age that affected parts of Scotland in the Permian Era. Glacial sediments occur in Brazil that were formed during the Carboniferous and Permian Periods (355–250 million years ago).

● **As glaciers and ice sheets move**, they pick up fresh and eroded rock material. This is carried in, on and beneath the ice. As the ice melts, deposition occurs.

● **A feature of many glacial sedimentary rocks** is that they are badly sorted. Within one deposit there will be fragments of many sizes, from fine clay to large boulders.

● **Glacial rocks are commonly un-bedded**. They do not have the neat strata that identify most sedimentary rocks.

● **The term moraine is used** to cover a wide variety of glacial deposits. It may consist of sand, gravel, clay and rock fragments. Much eroded rock debris falls along the sides of a glacier. This lateral moraine may be further eroded against the valley sides as the ice moves.

● **A push moraine is bulldozed** along at the glacier snout (front end). Any glacier may produce a number of these as it retreats and then re-advances. Terminal moraines usually form in this way, and give geologists evidence about the furthest position a glacier reached.

● **If two valley glaciers join**, their lateral moraines will merge to form a medial moraine in the new glacier.

● **Much meltwater is associated** with glaciers. This flows out from under the ice carrying sediment. Usually meltwater is thick and milky-looking because of the clay it contains. The area in front of the glacier snout is called an outwash plain. Water-formed sediments occur here, often in neat strata.

● **The large boulders carried** and dumped by the ice are often left stranded and out of place. These are called erratics, and their significance is considerable. By studying them, geologists can tell from where a long-vanished ice sheet came.

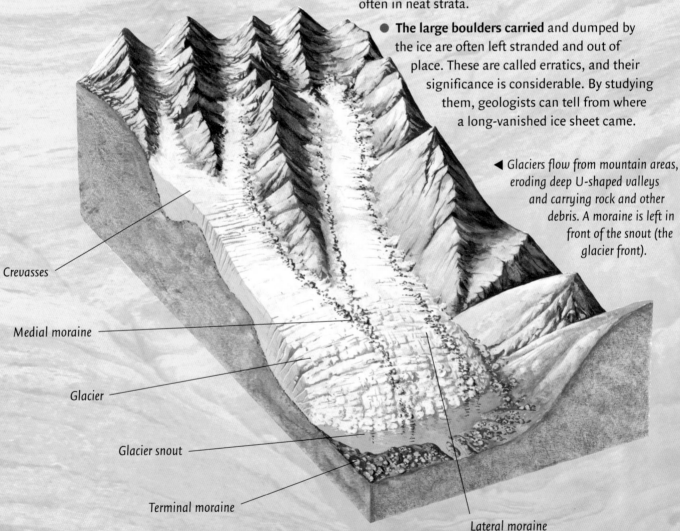

◄ *Glaciers flow from mountain areas, eroding deep U-shaped valleys and carrying rock and other debris. A moraine is left in front of the snout (the glacier front).*

Crevasses

Medial moraine

Glacier

Glacier snout

Terminal moraine

Lateral moraine

Coal

- **The fossil fuel coal is abundant** and easy to recover.

- **Coal is the remains** of carbon stored in plants. These plants, living hundreds of millions of years ago, took energy from sunlight and stored it in their tissues.

- **Coal is most common in strata** of the Carboniferous Period (355–298 million years ago).

- **Coal from the Jurassic Period** (208–144 million years ago) has been mined in England, north-east Scotland, Siberia and China.

- **The coal-forming plants** of the Carboniferous Period developed from peat deposited in the sedimentary layers of sand and mud formed on a vast delta.

- **Peat is the first stage** in the development of coal. It is formed from partially decayed plant matter.

- **As peat is buried under sediment**, it becomes compressed and heated. The heat drives off impurities. Gradually, the amount of carbon in the peat increases, it becomes (brown) lignite and then coal.

- **In some places**, peat is used for heating. It is burnt in power stations in some countries, such as Ireland.

- **Bituminous coal contains** much more carbon than lignite and is the most widely used coal.

- **At the present rate of use**, coal will long outlast oil and gas as a fossil fuel resource.

▼ *Dead vegetation forms peat as it slowly rots. After being buried and heated under thousands of kilometres of rock, the peat turns to coal.*

Peat accumulates as the trees die and decay slowly

With further burial, lignite or brown coal is formed

After the lignite has been buried deep underground, bituminous coal forms

Oil and gas

- **Oil and gas are fossil fuels.** Natural gas has mostly taken over from coal gas as a domestic and industrial fuel.

- **Oil has given wealth** to many poor nations.

- **Oil is a mixture** of many different hydrocarbons (compounds made of hydrogen and carbon) derived from marine organisms.

- **Oil and gas are very mobile** and move, through strata, away from where they were formed.

- **Usually, oil and gas are 'trapped'** below ground. They move upwards through porous or permeable strata like limestone.

- **Oil and gas may leak out** onto the Earth's surface making it easier to locate.

◄ *Significant reserves of oil and gas have been discovered in the rock under the seabed. The fossil fuel is obtained using oil rigs.*

- **Oil does not always flow up to the surface**, and so it is pumped to the surface by machines called 'nodding donkeys'.

- **When geologists start** prospecting for oil, they detect porous strata below the surface by measuring the electrical resistance of rocks or their reaction to shock waves from small explosions.

- **Most oil is discovered** by drilling boreholes. Drilling for oil requires a lubricant called drilling mud, which keeps the drill bit cool.

- **In some areas such as the North Sea**, oil was not found in the areas first prospected. Gas was present, however, and this became an important resource in the 1960s.

Evaporite rocks

● **The term 'evaporite' is used** for a range of rocks deposited from salt water, such as rock salt (halite), rock gypsum and potash.

● **The main evaporite deposits are formed** from minerals in sea water.

● **If part of the sea,** such as a bay, is cut off from the open ocean, it will begin to dry up. This is the start of evaporite formation.

● **Some evaporite deposits occur** where inland salt lakes have dried out.

● **In the sea,** a series of evaporite rocks are deposited in a definite sequence, usually interbedded with mudstone.

● **Some evaporite chemicals are more soluble** in water than others. The least soluble form layers of rock first.

● **Many evaporite deposits are forming** at the present time, especially in arid regions. These are usually processed where they occur.

● **Of the marine evaporates,** rock salt (halite) is essential for human and animal health. It has been in great demand for thousands of years as a food enhancer and preserve.

● **The evaporites deposited in land-bound lakes** include borax and nitrates. Borax is used in glass, paper and leather products. Nitrates are the basis of fertilizers, explosives and nitric acid.

● **In Britain there are considerable evaporite deposits.** Other important deposits are in Germany, the USA and Chile.

◄ Potash is used for making agricultural fertilizers. This mine, in the North York Moors National Park, is over 5 km deep.

Stalactites and stalagmites

● **Many limestone caves are covered** with hanging, icicle-shaped growth. These are called stalactites.

● **Limestone is easily weathered**. Acid rainwater changes the calcite in limestone into soluble calcium bicarbonate.

● **Chemical weathering of limestone** allows water to run underground. Passages are eroded by this water, forming cave systems.

● **In the British Isles,** limestone caves have been formed in north-west Scotland, Derbyshire, North Yorkshire, Gloucestershire, Devon and western Ireland.

● **The opening on the surface** down which water runs is called a pot hole. Gaping Gill pothole in North Yorkshire is 120 m deep.

◄ Straw stalactites develop where water rich in calcium bicarbonate seeps through small openings in a cave roof.

● **Water dripping from a limestone cave roof** is full of dissolved calcium bicarbonate. This is deposited as calcium carbonate (calcite) as the water drips into the cave and in part evaporates. The calcite is deposited in concentric rings to form stalactites.

● **Stalagmites usually form** beneath a stalactite from water dripping off its tip.

● **Stalactites that hang** from a cave roof tend to be slender. Some, known as straw stalactites, are small, but some are huge and can grow to many metres in length.

● **Both structures are made** of many layers of calcite. If cut open, the concentric rings of calcite can be seen.

★ STAR FACT ★
In western Ireland, a stalactite has been found that is 6.3 m long.

Superposition

● **Geology, like any science**, has a number of laws, or principles, which help scientists to interpret rocks. The principle of superposition is one of these.

● **William Smith (1769–1839), an English canal engineer** and pioneering geologist, established the principle of superposition.

● **In simple terms**, the law of superposition states that in a sequence of sedimentary rocks, the older rocks lie below the younger layers.

● **A geologist in the field** may have problems interpreting strata according to this principle. In extreme conditions, folding for example will overturn the beds of rock so that younger layers lie beneath older ones.

● **Similarly a 'thrust fault' may force** old rocks above younger ones, which is another reason why the principle cannot be applied.

● **There are a number of ways** in which a geologist can prove if rocks are the correct 'way up'. These need to be applied before the order of strata can be determined.

● **Each stratum marks a break** in the deposition of sediment. On its surface various marks may be made. These prove which way up it formed.

● **The sediment may be rippled**, like a modern beach. If sediment dried out, mud cracks would be formed.

● **Fossils of animals**, such as mollusc shells in their burrows, can also be used to show whether the rocks are the correct way up.

● **Volcanic rocks that contained** much gas will have their vesicles (gas-bubble holes) at the top of a lava flow.

▼ On this wave-cut platform, the older strata are closer to the sea and youngest ones on the land. Each stratum dips (slopes) towards the land and disappears below a younger (higher) layer.

Deltas

● **A delta is a mass of sediment** built up at the mouth of a river where it enters a lake or the sea.

● **The Mississippi Delta** in the Gulf of Mexico, USA, has built up 'fingers' of low-lying land. Here, there is little tide or wave energy to move the sediment.

● **Sediment is deposited** when a river enters deep water because its speed and power to transport sediment suddenly decreases.

● **Deltaic rocks include** mudstones and sandstones. Coal seams may be found in deltaic rocks.

● **As the top of a delta** is very close to sea level, a very slight increase in the sea level will cause flooding.

● **Millions of people live and work** on the Ganges and Brahmaputra delta region of north-east India and Bangladesh. Monsoon rains and storms in the Bay of Bengal often inundate the low-lying delta, with devastating results.

● **Many major oilfields are in ancient delta rocks.** These include the oilfields of Nigeria, the southern USA and the North Sea.

● **The building of the Aswan Dam** in Egypt has prevented sediment entering the Nile delta.

● **The marsh and water habitats found on** many deltas are home to a great variety of wildlife.

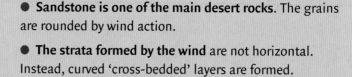

◀ The Nile delta has many distributary channels between which are low lying areas of fertile river sediment called alluvium.

Desert rocks

● **Deserts are arid regions** that receive very low rainfall, usually not enough to support vegetation.

● **Most desert regions are areas** of high temperatures, but Antarctica is also a desert.

● **By studying the sediments** and other features of today's deserts, geologists can work out which rocks were formed in ancient deserts.

▶ Rocks formed in arid areas are often red or orange coloured. Here, in the Arches National Park, USA, the strata have been weathered and eroded into pillars and cliffs.

● **Sandstone is one of the main desert rocks.** The grains are rounded by wind action.

● **The strata formed by the wind** are not horizontal. Instead, curved 'cross-bedded' layers are formed.

● **Larger fragments of quartz are often pitted** and frosted by sand blasting.

● **Deserts are very windy environments**, so mica, a mineral that occurs in small flakes, is absent from desert rocks.

● **If rain does fall on a desert region**, it is usually very heavy for a short time. This creates flash floods, which can carry sand, pebbles and boulders.

● **'Desert rose' is a flower-like formation** of the mineral gypsum that forms in deserts.

Concretions and nodules

● **Concretions and nodules are rounded** masses of rock found in many sedimentary rocks. They commonly occur in rows following the strata.

● **Most concretions are a few centimetres** in diameter, but some are measured in metres.

● **When they occur in mudstone**, concretions may be made of pyrite (iron sulphide), iron (siderite), calcite or phosphate.

● **Sandstone often contains** concretions that may be rich in iron compounds.

● **Flint forms as nodules** in the Cretaceous chalk. These dark masses are easily seen against the white rock.

● **Concretions are often made** of the same material in which they occur. They probably form after the sediment has been deposited, as it is turning to rock.

● **In some strata**, especially the lower Jurassic mudstones, concretions can contain well-preserved fossils. These are mainly molluscs such as ammonites.

● **A septarian nodule**, or concretion, is filled with radiating or concentric veins of mineral, often calcite.

● **The veins occupy** shrinkage cracks created as the nodules dry out.

● **Concretions and nodules** are usually more resistant to erosion than the mudstone in which they often occur.

◄ These rounded nodules in a Jurassic shale cliff are about 20 cm across. Often nodules such as these follow a particular stratum.

Metamorphic rocks

● **Metamorphic rocks** are any rocks that have been changed by heat, pressure or a combination of these forces.

● **Most metamorphic changes occur** at temperatures of between 200°C and 700°C.

● **Contact metamorphism involves** only heat. Regional metamorphism is brought about by heat and pressure.

● **No melting of rock occurs** during metamorphism. When melting takes place, magma, from which igneous rocks are formed, is created.

● **The chemical composition and structure** of a rock can be changed by metamorphism.

● **When large-scale faulting occurs**, dislocation metamorphism takes place.

◄ Garnet is a mineral that forms in many metamorphic rocks, especially schist. It is used as a semi-precious gemstone and may be cut and facetted.

● **Original structures**, such as strata in sedimentary rocks, are removed during metamorphism.

● **Fossils are sometimes found** in slightly metamorphosed rocks such as slate. As the degree of metamorphism increases, fossils are destroyed.

● **Garnet, a mineral much used** as a semi-precious gemstone, is common in the metamorphic rock called schist.

● **Some of the oldest rocks** in the Earth's crust are highly metamorphosed gneisses.

Contact metamorphism

- **Contact metamorphism occurs** when rocks are heated by magma or lava.

- **A metamorphic aureole is the region** around a mass of magma in which rocks have been altered.

- **A lava flow can only metamorphose** the rocks lying below it.

- **The amount of contact metamorphism depends** on the size of the igneous body producing heat and any fluids seeping from it.

- **The metamorphic aureole around a large batholith** may be a few kilometres wide.

- **A small sill, dyke or lava flow** may metamorphose rocks up to only a few centimetres away.

- **A gradual metamorphic change takes place** away from the igneous intrusion. The rocks furthest away are only slightly metamorphosed.

- **Dark-coloured 'spots' and clusters of minerals** are a common feature of clay and shale that have been altered by contact metamorphism.

- **When heated, limestone becomes** crystalline marble.

- **Sandstone is changed** to a hard, crystalline rock called metaquartzite.

▼ *The sloping rock surface on the right is made of granite. The dark hornfels are on the left of the picture. The contact between the two different rocks is clearly seen.*

Marble

- **Marble is formed** by the contact metamorphism of limestone.

- **Heat from an igneous intrusion** or lava flow causes the calcite in the limestone to recrystallize.

- **Original features in the limestone**, such as strata and fossils, are destroyed, and an interlocking mosaic of calcite crystals forms.

- **Pure limestones become very pale**, often sugary, marbles, with very little colour veining.

- **Limestone that has impurities** in the form of clay, other sedimentary material, or minerals, are changed into colourfully veined marbles.

- **The metamorphic minerals brucite, olivine, and serpentine** can give marble a greenish colouring.

- **Olivine marble has small patches** of bright green or brown olivine. This is a silicate mineral formed by the heat of metamorphism.

- **For over 2500 years**, marble has been prized as a decorative stone. This is because it is easily shaped and polished, and has attractive colouring.

- **In the classical Greek and Roman periods**, marble was the main rock used for statues.

- **Michelangelo's David**, carved between 1501 and 1504, is one of the most well-known marble statues in existence.

◀ *The abandoned marble quarry on the Isle of Iona, western Scotland. Marble was quarried here and much was shipped to Europe. This quarry closed in 1914.*

Metaquartzite

- **When sandstone is altered** by contact metamorphism, it turns into metaquartzite.

- **Heat from an igneous intrusion or lava flow causes** the quartz grains in sandstone to grow and fuse together or recrystallise.

- **Metaquartzite may have only faint traces** of the original bedding. Any fossils in the original sandstone will have been destroyed.

- **Sandstone is more resistant** to metamorphic change than many other rocks because so much heat is needed to alter it.

- **Metaquartzite is a pale-coloured rock**, often with a sugary texture.

▶ Originally sandstone, this metaquartzite is now a mosaic of quartz crystals. The original layers in the rock have disappeared.

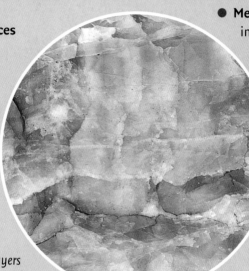

- **Sandstone is a porous rock** with small spaces between the grains. Metaquartzite is crystalline and non-porous.

- **As it is largely made of quartz**, metaquartzite is a very hard rock. It is resistant to weathering.

- **Metaquartzite is quarried** and used in the construction industry.

- **Metaquartzite is found** very close to large batholiths. Smaller intrusions rarely have sufficient heat to change quartz-rich sandstone.

- **Although it is virtually 100 percent quartz**, metaquartzite may contain feldspar and iron oxides in small amounts.

Crushed rock

- **Large-scale faulting causes rocks** along the fault surface to be crushed and metamorphosed.

- **Fault breccia is a rock** made of angular broken fragments. It is common along many fault lines.

- **The crushed rock formed** when thrust faults move deep in the Earth's crust is called mylonite.

- **Mylonite is made from** the dusty rock 'flour' that is created as rocks are ground up along the fault plane. Larger fragments, often stretched out, are stuck into this.

- **If thrust faults occur** deep in the crust where temperatures are high, new minerals will grow in mylonite. Chlorite, mica, feldspar and epidote are common examples.

- **As the fault moves**, rock flour and minerals are stretched out to give mylonite its typical texture.

- **Mylonite tends to break** in thin plates and slabs parallel to its texture.

- **Geologists use the term** 'cataclasis' for the processes that create mylonite.

- **Large-scale thrust faults occur** in areas of mountain building.

- **There are a number of thrust faults**, with associated mylonite, in the north-west Highlands of Scotland.

◀ The Glencoul thrust fault, Sutherland, Scotland. The thrust plane is the sloping surface halfway up the hillside. The grey mass of rock above it has moved from the right along the thrust plane above younger rocks.

Faulting

- **Faults are breaks** in the rocks of the Earth's crust where the rocks move relative to each other. The same stratum will be at a different level on each side of the fault.

- **A joint is a break in the rocks** where no movement takes place.

- **Both faults and joints are often the places** where hot, mineral-rich fluids rise through the crust.

- **The actual surface where the rocks break** and move is called the fault plane. In many faults, the fault plane is very steep.

- **When faults move**, earthquakes occur. Movement on the San Andreas Fault that runs through California, USA, threatens large cities such as Los Angeles.

- **A normal fault is where the Earth's crust** stretches and one mass of rock moves down a break – the fault plane.

◄ *Unlike most faults, the San Andreas Fault in California is visible on the Earth's surface.*

- **If two normal faults occur** parallel to each other a block of the crust may sink between them. This is called a rift, or graben.

- **Where a reverse fault occurs**, the Earth's crust is made thicker by compression. One mass of rock is forced up the fault plane relative to the rocks on the other side.

- **In a tear fault**, there is virtually no vertical movement. Rock masses are moved sideways relative to each other.

> ★ STAR FACT ★
> A thrust fault can move huge masses of rock many tens of kilometres up a very low angled fault plane.

Regional metamorphism

- **As the name implies**, this type of metamorphism occurs over great areas of the Earth's crust.

- **Regional metamorphism happens** when mountain building, often associated with movement of the Earth's lithospheric plates, occurs.

- **Pressure and heat are involved** in altering rocks by regional metamorphism.

- **The changes that take place** during regional metamorphism may take tens of millions of years to occur.

- **Some of the oldest rocks** in the Earth's crust have been affected by regional metamorphism. These have been radiometrically dated at over 3500 million years old.

▶ *Gneiss is formed by regional metamorphism – extreme heat and pressure deep within the Earth's crust.*

- **The deeper into the crust** that rocks are taken by the processes of mountain building, the higher the degree, or grade, of metamorphism they suffer.

- **Rocks formed by regional metamorphism** are identified by their texture. Due to stresses in the rock, minerals are streaked out in layers.

- **High-grade rocks** – those that are altered most – are called gneiss. With increased temperature, caused by depth of burial, melting may occur and magma is created.

- **At lower depths**, where the temperature and pressure are lower, a rock called schist is formed.

- **Around the margins of the mountain region**, temperatures are very low. Here, pressure is also low and rocks such as slate are created.

Slate

◀ *This specimen of slate contains crystals of pyrite (iron sulphide). Pyrite often forms during regional metamorphism. The rock has broken along a cleavage surface.*

● **Slate forms around the margins** of mountain regions where the lowest grade of regional metamorphism occurs.

● **Slates are dark-coloured rocks** made of grains and crystals too small to be seen with the naked eye.

● **The most recognizable feature of slate** is its cleavage. This is the way the rock splits into thin, neat layers. However, the most weakly metamorphosed slates may not have developed a cleavage.

● **As it splits so easily**, slate has been used for hundreds of years for roofing and gravestones.

● **Fossils may still be present in slate**. These are often squashed by the stresses that metamorphosed the rock.

● **Slate forms from the weak metamorphism** of mudstone or siltstone.

● **Small, golden-coloured crystals of pyrite** (fool's gold) form in some slates.

● **Green slate is coloured** by the mineral chlorite, which grows under metamorphic stress.

● **Some of the world's most important slate quarries** are in North Wales. Slate from here has been shipped all over the world.

● **Slate is also found in other parts of Britain**, including Cumbria, Scotland and Devon. Elsewhere in the world, it occurs in California, USA, Onijarvi, Finland and Vosges, France.

Schist

● **Schist forms at higher temperatures** and pressures than slate. These conditions occur deeper in the Earth's crust and nearer the centre of a mountain region.

● **Schist is a silvery rock** because it contains mica – this may be pale muscovite or dark biotite mica.

● **A typical feature of schist is a wavy banding** (called schistosity) running through the rock. This results from the way minerals have lined up during metamorphism.

● **As well as mica**, this rock contains quartz and feldspar.

● **Many new minerals can form** in schist during metamorphism. These include garnet, kyanite, hornblende and epidote.

◀ *The hills and mountains of the Scottish Highlands are largely made of schist.*

● **As temperatures and pressure are moderately high** when schists form, most rocks are altered.

● **Garnet schists are a source** of the semi-precious gemstone, garnet.

● **Much schist occurs in the European Alps**. Here, the rocks were folded and metamorphosed in mid-Cenozoic times, around 40 million years ago.

● **In Britain, schist occurs** mainly in the Scottish Highlands, where it was formed during the Caledonian Period of mountain building, around 400 million years ago.

● **A period of mountain building** is called an orogeny.

Gneiss

- **Gneiss is a rock formed** by extreme heat and pressure deep within the Earth's crust.

- **Under these conditions any previously formed rock** will be completely changed. This is the highest grade of regional metamorphism.

- **During orogenies**, some rocks are buried to the depths at which gneiss forms.

- **Gneiss is characterized** by alternating dark and light coloured bands of different minerals.

- **The darker streaks contain denser minerals** such as mica, while the pale bands contain lower-density minerals such as quartz.

- **Some gneisses may have isolated patches** of other minerals such as red garnet.

- **The composition of gneiss** is not very different from that of the igneous rock granite.

- **Gneiss is generally the oldest rock in the area** in which it occurs, and some gneisses have been radiometrically dated to over 3000 million years.

- **The major continental shield areas**, such as the Canadian and Eurasian shields, are predominantly made of gneiss, with younger rocks on top.

- **Gneiss is a very durable rock**. Its hardness is exploited in road making, and millions of tonnes of quarried gneiss boulders are used for coastal defences.

◀ Gneiss forms a rugged landscape of low grey hills with much bare rock.

Eclogite

- **Eclogite is a rock that forms** under high temperature and very high pressure in the deep roots of mountain chains.

- **It is a rare rock and is important** because of what geologists can learn from it about the Earth's composition.

- **Eclogite contains large crystals** easily seen with the naked eye.

- **The minerals in this rock** may be arranged in alternating bands of different types or randomly scattered throughout its structure.

- **Eclogite is a dark-coloured rock** made of yellowish or green pyroxene and red garnet.

▶ Eclogite can be a most attractive rock, with masses of red garnet and green pyroxene. This example is from Norway.

- **Other minerals that occur** in small amounts in eclogite include rutile, pyrite, corundum and kyanite.

- **Some eclogites are found in diamond pipes**. They have been taken there from great depth by volcanic activity.

- **Geologists believe that eclogite gives** important information about the rocks at the very base of the Earth's crust, and in the uppermost region of the Earth's mantle.

- **Experiments have shown that eclogite forms** when basalt lava is melted and recrystallized under great pressure.

- **Eclogite occurs worldwide**, especially in California, USA, the European Alps, Japan and South Africa.

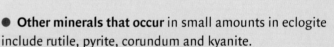

Building stones

- **Local stone is used for building.** It is often possible to work out what the local geology is like by looking at what buildings are made from.

- **Some rock types are especially sought after** because they are attractive, or easily cut into usable shapes.

- **Sandstone, limestone and ironstone are three sedimentary rocks** that are often used for building. Most of these can be cut easily and split along bedding planes.

- **Though granite is more difficult to cut** than some sedimentary rocks, it has been quarried for building stone for hundreds of years.

- **As stone used for buildings is often cut in large blocks,** quarries developed in the 18th and 19th centuries were usually near good transport facilities.

◄ *The body of this cottage is made of flint, found in nearby chalk strata.*

- **The famous Aberdeen granite quarries** and the granite quarries in the Channel Isles and Cornwall were often sited near to the sea to make it easy to transport the quarried rock.

- **Warm-coloured limestones are used** in southern England for many buildings.

- **Limestone is readily attacked** by chemical weathering, and many buildings need restoration work when the stone suffers.

- **Slate is a tough,** easily split rock used for roofing.

- **Polished stone often decorates** the facades of offices and banks. Usually, granite is used for this purpose.

What are minerals?

- **A mineral is a chemical compound** or element that forms naturally in many different ways.

- **Most minerals form inorganically,** which means that living things play no part in their creation. However, some organic materials, such as amber, are usually classed with minerals.

- **Rocks are made from minerals.** Limestone is made mainly of the mineral calcite (calcium carbonate), and granite contains quartz, mica and feldspar.

- **Some minerals,** such as gold and diamond, are very valuable as currency or gemstones.

- **Geologists tell one type of mineral** from another by using special tests. Many of these are easy to carry out.

- **Many minerals form as perfect crystals.** There is a great variety of crystal shapes, from simple cubes to complex dodecahedra with twelve faces.

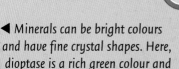

◄ *Minerals can be bright colours and have fine crystal shapes. Here, dioptase is a rich green colour and the crystals have a vitreous (glassy) lustre.*

- **Minerals can form irregular or rounded shapes** without obvious crystals.

- **Some minerals are magnetic,** others react with acids, and some are too hard to be scratched with a knife blade.

- **As well as occurring in rocks,** minerals form in long narrow bands, called mineral veins, which run through the Earth's crust.

- **Minerals such as hematite** (iron oxide), galena (lead sulphide) and salt (sodium chloride) are important industrial raw materials.

How hard are minerals?

● **Geologists use a number of tests** to tell one mineral from another. The hardness test is very useful when identifying minerals.

● **The hardness of a mineral depends** on the strength of the forces that bind the atoms in the mineral together.

● **Gemstones, such as diamond**, ruby, sapphire and emerald, are very hard. It is difficult to scratch or damage them.

● **Mineral hardness is measured** according to how easily a mineral can be scratched. A mineral is tested by scratching it in turn with objects of increasing hardness, including the minerals on the hardness scale.

● **Geologists use a special scale** for measuring mineral hardness. It is called Mohs scale and was devised in 1812 by the German mineralogist Friedrich Mohs. There are ten points on Mohs scale, each one defined by a well-known mineral.

● **Talc is the softest mineral** at point 1 on the hardness scale. One form of this mineral is called soapstone and can be easily carved into ornaments. It can be scratched with a fingernail.

● **Diamond is the hardest on the scale**, at point 10. This highly prized gemstone is so hard that it is also used in industry as a cutting tool.

● **The other minerals on the scale** are gypsum (2), calcite (3), fluorite (4), apatite (5), orthoclase (6), quartz (7), topaz (8) and corundum (9).

● **Certain everyday objects are also used** for testing hardness. A fingernail (2.5), coin (3.5) and knife blade (5.5) are often used.

> ★ STAR FACT ★
> The first nine minerals on Mohs scale have roughly the same gap between them – that is, corundum is nine times harder than talc. Diamond, however, the tenth mineral on the scale, is 40 times harder than talc.

1	2	3	4	5
Talc	Gypsum	Calcite	Fluorite	Apatite

6	7	8	9	10
Orthoclase	Quartz	Topaz	Corundum	Diamond

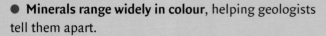

Mineral colours

- **Minerals range widely in colour**, helping geologists tell them apart.

- **Mineral colour depends on** how light is reflected and absorbed by the elements in the mineral.

- **Quartz, a very common mineral**, can occur in many different colours. Amethyst is purple, citrine is yellow and the pink form is called rose quartz. Usually, quartz is grey or milky white.

- **Malachite, which is a copper mineral**, is a rich green colour. Azurite, another mineral containing copper, is bright blue in colour.

- **Common minerals such as calcite**, gypsum and barite are usually white.

- **Minerals that contain iron**, such as hematite and magnetite, are often reddish-brown or black.

- **Gold is a wonderful rich yellow colour**. Fool's gold (pyrite) is a similar colour, as is copper pyrite (chalcopyrite). It is easy to tell them apart using other tests such as hardness and specific gravity.

- **Cinnabar, a sulphide of mercury**, is red, as is realgar (arsenic sulphide).

- **For thousands of years**, mineral colours have been used as pigment in paints and dyes. Malachite was used as a green pigment over 2000 years ago in Egypt.

- **Ultramarine, a rich deep-blue colour**, is made from powdered lazurite (lapis lazuli).

◀ *The brilliant green coating on this rock surface is the copper mineral conichalcite. Many minerals that contain copper are green.*

Gemstones

- **Gemstones have been prized** for thousands of years for their rarity, colour, shape and durability.

- **There are only a few dozen types of gemstones** in everyday circulation. Other gemstones are too rare or soft to be of much use.

- **Semi-precious gemstones include** many colour varieties of quartz, such as purple amethyst.

- **Gemstones form naturally** in many different geological situations. Some occur in igneous rocks, others in mineral veins or cavities.

- **Due to of their hardness**, gems such as ruby and sapphire are not worn away by erosion in a river and so accumulate in river gravels and sands. These forms of corundum have been weathered and eroded from their original source.

- **To enhance their natural beauty**, and remove imperfections, gemstones are cut and surfaces called facets are made.

- **Diamond is the best-known gemstone**. Imitation diamonds have been made for many years. Rock crystal (quartz) and glass have both been used, but today materials such as cubic zirconia are produced as diamond substitutes.

- **A person who cuts and polishes gemstones** is called a lapidary.

- **Gemstones, especially diamonds**, are measured in 'carats'. A carat is a measure of weight, being 0.2 g.

◀ *Small crystals of topaz growing into a hollow in an igneous rock. Topaz crystals can be cut and facetted as gemstones.*

Precious metals

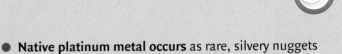

- **Gold, silver and platinum are all minerals** that are precious metals. They occur on their own as 'native elements', which means that they are not combined with other elements as compounds.

- **Gold is easily recognized** by its rich colour and great weight. It is 19 times heavier than an equal volume of water.

- **Gold is a soft metal**, easily scratched with a coin.

- **Found in a variety of geological situations**, gold occurs in veins, often with quartz. It occurs in river sand and shingle, where prospectors 'pan for gold'.

- **Native platinum metal occurs** as rare, silvery nuggets and minute grains with nickel and gold.

- **Platinum commands a higher price** on the world market than gold. It is used in catalytic converters, oil refining and jewellery.

- **Silver is far less valuable than gold or platinum.** When clean, it has a fine metallic lustre, but this rapidly fades and the metal becomes dull.

- **Silver forms in delicate twisted wire shapes.** Today, most silver is obtained from lead and copper mining, and refining.

- **As well as being used to make jewellery** and ornaments, silver is a component of photographic film.

◀ *Gold is often found in quartz veins. This fine crystal of quartz has small flakes of gold on its surfaces.*

Mining

▶ *Bauxite is an important ore of aluminium. This metal is strong and lightweight and does not rust like steel.*

- **The metals and fuels on which we depend** are mined or quarried from the ground.

- **Rock that contains valuable material**, usually metal, is called an ore. Hematite is an iron ore and bauxite is an ore of aluminium.

- **Over 3000 million tonnes of metal** and mineral ores are mined each year.

- **Ores are finite, non-renewable materials.** It is therefore important to recycle metals after use.

- **Metal ores exist in many different geological settings.** How they are mined largely depends on the size and shape of the deposit.

- **If an ore body is large** and occurs at depth in rocks that are structurally strong, an underground mine will be used.

- **Surface (open pit) mining** is cheaper to carry out than underground mining. It can also produce far more ore in less time.

- **If the ore is in loose surface sediments**, it can be mined by using high-pressure water jets. Settling tanks may be used to separate the heavy ore from unwanted sand and clay.

- **Coal mining was once a major industry** in Britain, with hundreds of mines. Today, because of the low price of foreign coal and the use of other fuels, only a few mines are still working. Coal is also extracted by opencast methods.

- **Old mine workings and spoil heaps** are excellent places to look for mineral specimens, if care is taken and permission sought from the landowner.

Looking for minerals

- **Prospecting for mineral deposits** has become a refined science using advanced techniques. It still relies, however, on certain proved methods, including field mapping.

- **Field mapping involves mapping rock structures** on the ground. The use of aerial photography and satellite imagery is useful for seeing such structures.

- **Many mineral deposits are below ground.** These can be investigated using what are called geophysical methods.

- **Rocks and minerals have a property** called specific gravity. This can be measured from the surface.

- **Iron deposits often have a strong magnetism.** In the 17th century, prospecting for iron ores was done using a compass.

- **Modern magnetometers are so refined**, they can measure slight changes in magnetism.

- **Geochemical analysis of river sediment** will detect metals that occur in valuable concentrations in the rocks the river has eroded.

- **Using a scintillometer** (Geiger) counter in the field may indicate concentrations of radioactive minerals such as uraninite.

- **Mineral deposits may be weathered** and altered on the surface. Water that seeps underground can carry minerals and concentrate them at depth.

- **Gold, rubies and sapphires** found by panning in river sand may indicate the presence of more minerals upstream.

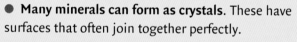

◄ This machine, called a cradle, was used to wash sand that may have contained gold. Heavy grains and nuggets of gold were left behind as the lighter sand was washed away.

Crystals

- **Many minerals can form as crystals.** These have surfaces that often join together perfectly.

- **Crystals show symmetry.** As a crystal is turned round, the same shape may be seen a number of times.

- **Mineralogists, scientists who study minerals and crystals,** classify crystals into a number of 'systems', according to their symmetry. The most symmetrical crystal system is called the cubic system.

- **Not all minerals that form within a certain system** will have the same crystal shape. In the cubic system there can be many shapes, including cubes and octahedra (eight-sided crystals). These shapes share the same symmetry.

- **The shape of a crystal results from the way** the atoms it is made of are fixed together.

> ★ STAR FACT ★
> In Brazil, giant specimens of rock crystal (quartz) have been found that are as big as a child.

- **Many rocks, especially igneous rocks**, are made of crystals of different minerals.

- **Some crystals are transparent** and allow light to pass completely through them.

- **The way the atoms of a crystal are arranged** may allow the crystal to break along a flat surface. This is called mineral cleavage.

- **Some crystals break with a rough surface.** This is known as mineral fracture.

◄ Rhodochrosite often forms in banded masses. This specimen shows flat, tabular crystals.

Other mineral shapes

● **The actual shape in which a mineral forms** is called its habit.

● **Mineral habit is a useful aid** to help in identifying minerals.

● **When a mineral forms no definite shape**, it is said to have a massive habit. Lots of minerals, such as quartz, have this habit. They can also be crystalline.

● **Rounded habits are common.** Hematite (iron oxide) often occurs as reniform (kidney-shaped) masses.

● **A botryoidal habit is like a bunch of grapes**, with many small, rounded structures. Malachite can occur like this.

● **Native metallic elements**, such as silver and copper, frequently form as wires. These can look like tree branches and this habit is called dendritic.

◀ This is not a fossil plant but delicate patterns formed by the mineral pyrolusite. This is known as a dendritic habit.

● **Minerals sometimes form in elongated masses** like stalactites. Goethite (an iron mineral) often has this stalactitic habit.

● **Well-formed crystals that have a constant shape** in cross-section are said to possess prismatic habit. A hexagonal quartz crystal is prismatic.

● **Mica crystals are flat and flaky**, rather like a table top. This habit is called tabular.

● **A habit that looks like a fossil coral** is called coralloidal. Aragonite (a form of calcium carbonate) sometimes occurs in this way.

Minerals in rocks

● **Minerals are everywhere.** All rocks contain minerals and many minerals form as magma cools to make igneous rocks.

● **The elements in the Earth's crust** combine to make minerals, but only eight elements are very common, and these account for over 90 percent of the crust.

● **The main mineral-forming elements are oxygen,** silicon, aluminium, iron, calcium, sodium, potassium and magnesium.

● **Oxygen and silicon are important rock-forming elements**, as they are the basis of silicate minerals.

● **As magma or lava cools**, silicate minerals form in a definite sequence. The dense, heavy minerals that crystallize at the highest temperatures form first.

● **Olivine is usually the first mineral to form**, followed by pyroxene and amphibole. Feldspars, micas and quartz also crystallize in igneous rocks.

◀ As igneous rock cools, minerals crystallize. In this basalt lava, olivine, pyroxene and feldspar will form as the molten rock solidifies.

● **Many sedimentary rocks contain minerals** that have been eroded from other rocks. Limestone contains calcite, which is formed for the first time in that rock.

● **Metamorphic rocks have a number of special minerals** in them. These include garnet, kyanite and mica.

● **Certain minerals** capitalize at low temperature on the Earth's crust. A group called 'evaporites' (which includes halite and gypsum) form as sea water dries.

★ STAR FACT ★
Some recently discovered minerals form in shipwrecks. Others form in blast furnace slag.

Mineral occurrence

- **Many of the finest mineral specimens** and some of the rarest minerals are found in mineral veins.

- **When rocks break because of tension** in the Earth's crust, faults and joints are formed. Hot fluids from great depths seep upwards into these cracks and deposit minerals. These fractures become mineral veins.

- **Hot mineral-forming fluids are called hydrothermal fluids** because they are rich in water.

- **Minerals containing important metals** such as galena (lead), sphalerite (zinc), chalcopyrite (copper) and cassiterite (tin) occur in mineral veins.

- **Other common hydrothermal vein minerals** are fluorite, calcite and quartz.

◀ A specimen of blue plumbogummite and yellowish pyromorphite. Countless tonnes of economically useful minerals come from veins.

- **Hydrothermal veins are often associated with** granite batholiths. Hot mineral-rich fluids may form after much of the magma has cooled.

- **Fluids from the Earth's crust** may be drawn upwards by heat and minerals can be deposited near granite.

- **A mineral vein looks like a gash** running through rocks. It is often white, containing quartz as the most common mineral.

- **Many minerals occur** in what are called placer deposits. These are concentrations of certain minerals in river sand and silt.

- **Only minerals that are durable** and heavy are found in placers. Gold, tin, platinum and diamonds occur in placers.

Quartz

- **Quartz is one of the most common minerals.** It is widespread and occurs in most rocks.

- **Quartz can be a great variety of colours.** Some of the colour forms are semi-precious gemstones. Amethyst (purple), rose quartz (pink), smoky quartz (black and dark brown) and citrine (orange) are all cut and polished for jewellery.

- **Quartz is the hardest common mineral.** It is the defining mineral at point 7 on the hardness scale, and cannot be scratched with a knife blade.

- **Agate, a semi-precious stone formed in concentric bands,** has the same chemical composition as quartz.

- **Chalcedony is a variety of quartz** made of microscopic crystals.

▶ Amethyst is the purple-coloured, semi-precious form of quartz.

★ STAR FACT ★
The largest quartz crystal was found in Brazil. It was 6 m long and weighed 48 tonnes.

- **Quartz often occurs** as magnificent crystals. These are six-sided (hexagonal) and usually have six triangular faces, forming a pyramid at the top.

- **Quartz is made of atoms of silicon and oxygen** in the form of silicon dioxide.

- **There are many ways in which quartz is used.** Small crystals of quartz are used in the mechanisms of watches and electronics equipment.

- **Colourless, transparent quartz** is called rock crystal.

Feldspar and mica

- **The group of minerals called feldspars** are the most common minerals in the Earth's crust. Feldspars are generally pale-coloured, though some are reddish, bluish or green.

- **Feldspar makes up** nearly half the composition of basalt lava, which covers the floor of the oceans.

- **Feldspar is a silicate mineral** containing silicon and oxygen. Different types of feldspar have atoms of different metallic elements.

- **Orthoclase feldspar is a silicate of potassium** and aluminium. This is common in granite.

- **Plagioclase feldspar has a variable composition.** It is a silicate of sodium and aluminium or calcium and aluminium. This feldspar mainly occurs in basalt and related rocks.

- **Feldspar is used in pottery glazes** and glass. It alters to china clay when decomposed.

- **Mica is a complex silicate** containing potassium, aluminium and iron.

- **Due to its very glittery appearance** and flaky habit, mica is easy to identify.

- **Mica is common in many igneous rocks**, especially granite.

- **Mica has good insulating properties** and is often powdered and used for this purpose.

▼ Feldspar is a very common mineral and is commonly white or pale-coloured. Amazonite is a brilliant blue-green variety, seen here as fine crystals.

▲ This glittery mass of mica has typically thin, flaky crystals. Pale-coloured mica is called muscovite.

Augite and hornblende

- **A member of the mineral group called pyroxenes**, augite is a silicate formed at high temperatures in magma and lava.

- **Augite is a dark, virtually black mineral** that helps to give rocks their dark colouring. It can also be brown or dark green.

- **Augite crystals are small,** prismatic and stubby.

- **Augite crystals make up about 50 percent of gabbro,** a coarse-grained igneous rock.

- **Hornblende is very like augite** in appearance. It belongs to the amphibole group of minerals.

- **A very dark-coloured mineral,** hornblende can be green, brown or black.

◄ Augite crystals tend to be short and stubby. When they break, rectangular shapes are formed, as in the large specimen on the left.

- **The crystals formed by hornblende** are long and prismatic, often with a fibrous appearance.

- **Hornblende forms in pale-coloured igneous rocks** such as granite and porphyry.

- **The metamorphic rock called amphibolite** contains hornblende.

- **When hornblende and augite break,** different angles are produced between the cleavage. Hornblende breaks with an angle of either 60° or 120° between them. Augite breaks with 90° between the surfaces.

Olivine

- **Olivine** crystallizes at very high temperatures in basalts and related rocks.

- **It is a greenish or brown mineral,** which occurs as small grains or crystals.

- **The colour of olivine varies** depending on its chemical composition. It is a silicate of iron and magnesium. An increase in iron content gives a browner colour.

- **One of the hardest rock-forming minerals,** olivine is almost as hard as quartz.

- **Meteorites found in Antarctica,** belonging to a group called 'stony-irons', are made of metal and the mineral olivine.

- **Due to its green colour and hardness,** fine crystalline olivine is used as a gemstone called peridot.

◄ Olivine can be cut and facetted as a gem stone. This small cut stone is surrounded by water-worn olivine crystals. Gem quality olivine is called peridot.

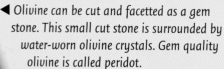

- **Gem-quality olivine comes mainly** from Arizona, USA, Myanmar (Burma) and Norway.

- **In basalt lava, olivine occurs** as bright green, rounded crystals studding the rock surface.

- **Peridotite, a rock which forms** very deep in the Earth's crust, is composed of garnet and olivine.

- **Dunite is an igneous rock** made almost entirely of olivine. It has a greenish-brown appearance.

Galena and cassiterite

- **Galena (lead sulphide) has been mined** since Roman times as an ore of lead.

- **A very dense mineral**, galena is made of lead sulphide, and is 7.5 times heavier than an equal volume of water.

- **Galena is a soft, grey-coloured mineral**, easily scratched with a coin. It crystallizes in the cubic system and is often found as near perfect cubes.

- **Lead was once used to make water and gas pipes** because it was easily bent to the correct shape. However, it fractures, and produces a cumulative poison that builds up in the body.

- **For thousands of years the county of Cornwall in the UK** was a source of tin, extracted from cassiterite (tin oxide).

- **This mineral occurs in hydrothermal veins**, often associated with large granite batholiths.

- **Cassiterite can be recognized** by its dark-brown or black colour and high density. It is a hard mineral – even a knife blade will not scratch it.

- **About 5000 years ago**, the Mesopotamians made bronze by adding tin to copper.

- **Pewter, used much in the past for drinking vessels**, is an alloy of tin and lead. Tin is used today in solder and tin plate.

- **Today lead is used in vehicle batteries** and as a shield against radioactive sources.

◀ *Today, one of the main uses of lead is for the plates in vehicle batteries. Lead is obtained from galena.*

Iron ores

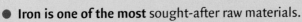

▼ *This 2000-year-old iron chain was found in a Welsh Lake called Llyn Cerrig Bach.*

- **Iron is one of the most** sought-after raw materials.

- **Many of the sedimentary iron ores** of the Jurassic Age in England are now composed of rusty coloured limonite. This resulted from the weathering of other iron minerals and concentrated the iron into sufficient quantities to make it workable. In the fresh state, many of these ores were not economic to work.

- **Most iron ore mined today** is found in sedimentary rocks. The richest deposits are in Labrador (Canada), Hamersley (Western Australia), near Lake Superior (USA), and in the Ukraine.

- **Hematite (iron oxide) is a rich ore**. It is a mineral with either a black or a reddish colour.

- **Hematite frequently occurs** in rounded, 'kidney ore' shapes. The crystalline form is called specularite.

- **As it contains iron**, hematite is a heavy mineral with a specific gravity 5.26 times heavier than water.

- **Magnetite is another rich source of iron**. It forms as black crystals or huge, irregular specimens. A hard mineral, it cannot be scratched by a knife blade.

- **As its name suggests**, magnetite is magnetic. This magnetism is strong enough to move a compass needle and attract iron filings.

- **Mountaineers and walkers in areas** where the rocks contain magnetite will find their compasses give inaccurate readings.

- **In Tenerife in the Canary Islands**, there are black magnetite sand beaches, made of iron ore that has been weathered out of lava.

Bauxite

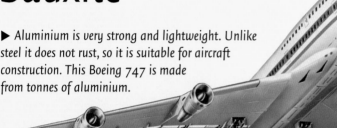

► *Aluminium is very strong and lightweight. Unlike steel it does not rust, so it is suitable for aircraft construction. This Boeing 747 is made from tonnes of aluminium.*

● **Some geologists argue** that bauxite is a rock, not a mineral, because it is a mixture of various materials. These include several oxides of aluminium.

● **Bauxite is usually formed** by the weathering of other rocks rich in silicates of aluminium. This happens mainly in tropical regions.

● **It is an attractive material**, orange or buff-coloured, containing red specks and patches.

● **As well as aluminium**, bauxite commonly contains some iron oxide.

● **Bauxite is a soft material**, easily scratched with a fingernail. It is also low density and is only 2.5 times heavier than water.

● **Mined for its aluminium content**, bauxite is the major source of this metal.

● **Aluminium conducts electricity well** and is lightweight.

● **It is obtained from its ore by electrolysis.** This involves the use of electricity – often low-cost hydroelectricity.

● **Aluminium is very resistant to corrosion**. It does not rust like iron and steel.

● **Due to its strength and light weight,** aluminium is used in the construction industry and increasingly in vehicle manufacture.

Diamond and graphite

● **Diamond and graphite are remarkably different forms** of the same element, carbon. The properties of these two forms of carbon result from the way their atoms are joined.

● **Many diamonds** may be over 3000 million years old.

● **Graphite is very soft** and is easily scratched with a fingernail.

● **Diamond forms small, glassy, often octahedral crystals** in the cubic crystal system and is the hardest known mineral.

● **Graphite forms in flat, platelike pieces** with a six-sided outline (hexagonal crystal system). These have a dull, greasy or metallic sheen.

● **The atoms in diamond** are joined in groups of five. These link together in a tight, close structure.

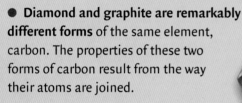

◄ *Diamond has been prized as a gemstone for thousands of years. This example has been cut and facetted to show off its sparkle.*

● **In graphite, the atoms are arranged in layers** or sheets that are weakly joined.

● **Diamond is much prized** as a gemstone and is also used for industrial cutting.

● **Graphite is used as pencil 'lead'.** The pencil industry in Keswick, UK, was based on local graphite.

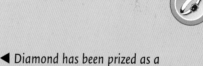

★ STAR FACT ★
Many diamonds were formed at a depth of 200 kilometres.

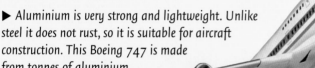

Birthstones

● **For nearly 2000 years**, crystals and precious stones have been linked with months of the year. Different religious and cultural groups have associated different stones with the months. The associations shown here are those popular in western culture today.

● **Garnet, a gemstone often with a rich, dark-red colour**, and found in metamorphic rocks, is the birthstone for January.

● **The birthstone for February** is amethyst. This is a purple, semi-precious form of quartz.

● **If you are born in March or May**, forms of beryl are your birthstones. March is represented by pale-blue aquamarine and May by green emerald.

● **The most valued gemstone**, diamond, is the birthstone for April.

● **June has an organic gemstone**, pearl, as its birthstone.

● **Ruby, the birthstone for July**, and sapphire, September's birthstone, are both forms of corundum, the second-hardest mineral.

● **A gem variety of the silicate mineral olivine**, called peridot, represents the month of August.

● **Opal, a gemstone with a rich play of colours**, which can change as the stone is heated, is the birthstone for October.

● **The third-hardest gemstone**, topaz, is the birthstone for people born in November. Turquoise, a rich blue gemstone, is linked with December.

▼ Each month of the year is characterized by a certain gemstone. The exact stones representing each month have not always been the same and those used in certain countries are different. The stones here are those generally used today.

December
Turquoise

January
Garnet

November
Topaz

February
Amethyst

October
Opal

March
Aquamarine

September
Sapphire

April
Diamond

August
Peridot

May
Emerald

July
Ruby

June
Pearl

Beryl and tourmaline

● **These two minerals are silicates** of various metals. They occur in igneous rocks such as granites and pegmatites.

● **Harder than quartz,** Beryl forms hexagonal crystals.

● **A number of colour varieties of beryl are known,** many of which are gemstones. Emerald is the rich green variety of beryl, heliodor is yellow, morganite is a pink form and aquamarine is greenish-blue.

● **Beryl can be translucent or transparent,** and has a glassy lustre (sheen).

● **In granites,** tourmaline forms black prismatic crystals. This type of tourmaline is called schorl.

● **With a hardness of 7,** tourmaline is as hard as quartz. It forms prismatic crystals and may be transparent.

● **There are more colour varieties of tourmaline** than of any other gemstone.

● **Rubellite is pink tourmaline,** and the green form is called elbaite. It can also be blue, yellowish and grey-blue.

● **Some tourmaline crystals are green** at one end and pink at the other.

▲ Some of the colour varieties of tourmaline.

★ STAR FACT ★
The largest crystal ever found was a beryl crystal discovered in Madagascar in 1976. It was 18 m long and weighed 380 tonnes.

Opal

● **Opal is a form of silicon dioxide,** but is chemically different from quartz as it contains water in its structure.

● **The silica in opal is packed together** in minute spheres. Opal is thus a non-crystalline mineral.

● **Opal occurs in many different forms.** It can be botryoidal (shaped like a bunch of grapes), reniform (kidney-shaped) or shaped like a stalactite.

● **Opal is a well-known gemstone,** though it is not of great hardness. Nevertheless, it has a number of attractive features.

● **Opal forms in certain volcanic rocks,** but also often around hot springs.

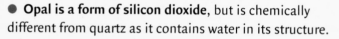

▶ This Australian opal shows typical colour variation from green to blue. Being translucent, light passes into the mineral and gives the colours depth.

★ STAR FACT ★
Fossilized trees are sometimes made of wood opal. This replaces the woody tissue perfectly.

● **Due to the packing of minute spheres** in the structure of opal, light is scattered to produce many colours. These vary from blue and green to red and pink. When heated, opal may change colour.

● **Another feature of gem opal** is the way it produces flashes of colour, which are best shown in curved, polished specimens called cabochons.

● **The Romans considered opal** to be a symbol of power and the Aztec civilization valued it as a gem.

● **Today, much of the world's opal** comes from Australia, but some also comes from Mexico.

Geodes and agates

- **A geode is a gas cavity (vesicle) in lava,** usually basalt, which has been filled in with minerals. Quartz in various forms is common in geodes.

- **Basalt lava erupts onto the Earth's surface** at over 1000°C. As it cools, gas is released and small cavities are left where the gas bubbles were trapped.

- **When basalt containing geodes is weathered,** the geodes, being very hard, are left behind. They often look like lumpy potatoes, but when cut open the wonderful coloured bands of agate are revealed.

- **In some geodes,** agate lines the cavity and delicate crystals grow into the hollow interior.

- **Agate is not made of crystalline quartz.** In an agate, the quartz is in minute fibres and grains.

- **Agate is one of the most varied semi-precious stones.** It occurs in many forms and colours.

- **A hard gemstone,** agate is translucent, and can be grey, blue, red, green or white.

- **Agate often occurs** in bands of different colours. These may be parallel (onyx) or concentric.

- **South American agates** from Uruguay and Brazil are the most common.

- **In Britain, agates can be found in many places.** Southern Scotland is the source of the best agates. They also occur in the Cheviot Hills in Northumberland, in Cornwall and on North Sea beaches.

◄ *This agate shows typical alternating colour bands. The specimen has been cut and polished.*

Native raw elements

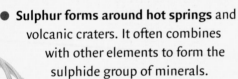

▶ *Native copper is used to make copper wire. This is a good conductor of electricity.*

- **As well as gold and diamond,** there are a number of other minerals that are important native elements.

- **Copper is a metal that occurs** as dendritic and shapeless, massive specimens. It is soft and easily scratched, but is very dense.

- **Copper also combines with other elements** in various minerals. One of its main uses is in electrical wiring.

- **Arsenic usually occurs as rounded,** botryoidal masses and can also be found in the form of grains.

- **A group of minerals called arsenates** contain arsenic combined with other elements. Arsenic is poisonous.

- **Sulphur is a bright yellow element** that can occur as fine pyramidal crystals.

- **Sulphur forms around hot springs** and volcanic craters. It often combines with other elements to form the sulphide group of minerals.

- **The element bismuth,** a silvery, metallic mineral that is soft but very dense, occurs in hydrothermal veins and pegmatites.

- **Bismuth also occurs** combined with sulphur as a mineral called bismuthinite.

> ★ **STAR FACT** ★
> Copper pins and beads have been discovered in the Middle East, dating back more than 7000 years.

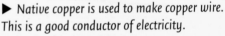

Radioactive minerals

● **There are a few minerals that contain uranium,** a dense, radioactive element.

● **Uranium combines with oxygen to form uraninite (pitchblende),** with copper, phosphorus and oxygen to form torbernite. It also combines with calcium, phosphorus and oxygen to make autunite.

● **Uranium is sought after as a source of fuel** for nuclear reactors. Other highly radioactive elements, such as plutonium, can be made from it.

● **Uraninite, or pitchblende, occurs as cube-shaped crystals** or in rounded masses. A very dense mineral, uraninite is up to ten times heavier than water.

● **Torbernite forms as bright green,** box-shaped crystals. These have a shiny surface.

● **Easily scratched with a coin,** torbernite forms by the alteration of uraninite by fluids in the Earth's crust.

● **Autunite is bright yellow or green** and occurs as small crystals and crusty masses.

● **Like torbernite, autunite is easily scratched** with a coin and is only of average density.

● **Radioactive minerals are only for expert use.** They have to be stored securely, often in lead-lined containers.

> ★ STAR FACT ★
> In 1898 the Polish scientist Marie Curie and her French husband Pierre discovered radioactivity. They identified the elements radium, potassium and helium in a specimen of pitchblende, a variety of uraninite. Radium from pitchblende is widely used in medicine and industry.

▼ By splitting uranium atoms, high levels of energy are produced. The atom's nucleus (centre), which makes up almost all of its mass, is made up of protons and neutrons. These are held together by a very strong force. By harnessing this force, nuclear energy is made.

Proton
Neutron
Electron

Toxic minerals

- **Many minerals are poisonous**. The two described here, orpiment and realgar, are sulphides of arsenic and can be dangerous. Due to their remarkable colours, they have been used as pigment in paint.

- **Orpiment is a wonderful golden yellow colour**. Indeed, it is so golden that hundreds of years ago, alchemists tried to extract gold from it.

- **Orpiment usually occurs in mineral veins** and around hot springs. Like many arsenic minerals, it smells of garlic when heated.

- **It has a resinous appearance** and forms thin, flaky pieces or small crystals.

- **The yellow paint pigment** made from orpiment is called 'King's Yellow'.

- **Realgar is found in the same geological situations** as orpiment. It has a very similar chemical composition, but is a vivid red colour.

- **Realgar has small, prismatic crystals**, which often have lines on their surfaces.

- **The surface of realgar has a greasy sheen**. It is a very soft mineral, easily scratched with a fingernail.

- **Orpiment and realgar** are readily available from mineral dealers. They are not dangerous if carefully stored and if hands are well-washed after handling specimens.

- **Over 3500 years ago**, the Egyptians used crushed realgar as a paint pigment.

◀ Paint pigments are often made from powdered minerals.

Fool's gold

- **There are many minerals that look like gold**. Small golden flecks of mineral in a stream bed may catch the eye but are often found not to be the real thing.

- **The two minerals generally referred to as fool's gold** are pyrite (iron sulphide) and chalcopyrite (copper iron sulphide).

- **With a few simple tests**, it is easy to tell real gold from other minerals.

- **Pyrite is a common mineral** in many geological situations. It occurs in mineral veins, metamorphic and sedimentary rocks, and in some igneous rocks.

- **Gold is a very soft mineral**, which can be scratched with a coin, but pyrite is harder than a knife blade.

- **The true colour of pyrite** is silvery yellow, not a rich deep yellow.

◀ Pyrite commonly occurs as fine, cube-shaped crystals which, as shown here, have striations (lines) on their faces.

- **Chalcopyrite** is a deeper yellow than pyrite and nearer to gold in colour. However, chalcopyrite tarnishes on exposure to air to give wonderful 'peacock' colours.

- **Chalcopyrite is softer than pyrite**, but harder than gold.

- **Both types of fool's gold** are not nearly as dense as true gold. An equal-sized specimen of gold would be far heavier than the impostors.

- **Chalcopyrite is a valuable mineral**, being a very important ore of copper.

Healing crystals

- **For thousands of years** a number of minerals have been associated with medicine and healing.

- **Early civilizations, including the Aztecs and Incas,** used crystals for their supposed ability to heal.

- **Quartz is thought to have great healing properties.** This may stem from its ability to vibrate consistently. A perfect quartz crystal can allow meditation at a deep level.

- **Sapphire, a form of corundum**, is believed to be a healing mineral. It is supposedly good for backache and skin disorders. It may also promote contentment and peace of mind.

- **Opal has had a mixed reception** as a healing mineral. It is claimed to induce daydreaming, which may not be a good thing.

- **Tourmaline is said to give confidence**, relieve nervousness and promote self-assurance.

- **In Taos, New Mexico,** the Crystal Academy has been set up to promote the use of crystals in healing.

- **Topaz is thought to relieve high blood pressure** and is also believed to cure insomnia.

- **Malachite, the bright green copper mineral,** may relieve asthma and depression.

- **It is not known how crystal healing works**. It may be related to light reflecting off the crystals having an effect on the body's electromagnetic field.

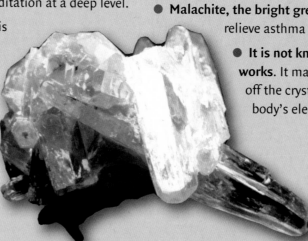

◀ Quartz crystals are supposed to have many healing properties.

Halite and gypsum

- **These minerals are both evaporites**, formed by the drying up of salt lakes and shallow seas. Halite is a chloride, and gypsum a sulphate.

- **Both minerals are of considerable economic importance**, being used in the chemical and construction industries.

- **Gypsum (hydrated calcium sulphate) is the basis** for the manufacture of plaster and plasterboard. It is also used in cement manufacture.

- **Halite, (sodium chloride) is used in the manufacture of soap**, dyes, caustic soda, insecticides and chlorine. It is also used for de-icing roads.

- **Large chemical industries are sited** in England and Germany, where concentrations of salt (halite) occurs.

- **Halite can be readily identified** by its salty taste. It is usually orange, grey or white in colour, but can be black.

- **As it is very soluble,** the cube-shaped crystals tend to lose their sharp edges unless they are kept in sealed, dry containers.

- **Halite is very soft,** and easily scratched with a fingernail.

- **Gypsum often occurs as fine crystals.** These can be diamond shaped or long and thin. A form called 'daisy gypsum' is like a rosette of tiny flowers.

- **Gypsum is the definition** of point 2 on the minerals hardness scale.

◀ One of the uses of halite is in the manufacture of soap.

Calcite and rhodochrosite

- **Calcite and rhodochrosite are both carbonate minerals.** They are made of a metal joined in a chemical compound with carbon and oxygen.

- **Calcite (calcium carbonate) is one of the most common minerals.** It is the main mineral in limestone, and metamorphic marbles are composed of calcite.

- **Hydrothermal veins often contain** calcite along with other minerals, such as galena, sphalerite and barite.

- **Calcite is uncommon in igneous rocks.** A group of volcanic and magmatic rocks called carbonatites are rich in carbonates. These are rare rocks usually found with syenite.

- **Calcite defines point 3** on the hardness scale. It forms as sharply pointed or flattened six-sided crystals.

- **Rhodochrosite (manganese carbonate) is a rich, deep pinkish-red colour.** Many minerals containing manganese are red.

- **Rhodochrosite can form as crystals**, but also occurs in rounded or nodular masses.

- **Both calcite and rhodochrosite** dissolve in hydrochloric acid (the acid needs to be warm to react with rhodochrosite). The bubbles given off are of carbon dioxide.

- **Rhodochrosite occurs** in hydrothermal veins and where rocks rich in manganese have been altered.

- **Due to its attractive colour,** rhodochrosite is cut and polished ornamentally.

◀ When calcite crystals have flattened tops they are called nail-head crystals.

Strange mineral properties

- **Due to their chemistry or crystal structure,** some minerals have certain properties that are special to them.

- **A transparent crystal of calcite** is called Iceland spar. When an object is seen through such a crystal, it appears double. This is called double refraction.

- **Many minerals react with acids.** Certain sulphides, such as galena, release hydrogen sulphide gas when reacting with hydrochloric acid.

- **Ruby, sapphire and some other minerals** contain minute criss-cross needles of rutile that produce a shining starshape when light shines on them. This optical property is known as asterism.

- **Some minerals containing iron** are magnetic. Hematite becomes magnetic when heated.

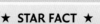

▶ Magnetite, as its name suggests, is magnetic.

★ STAR FACT ★
Chatoyancy produces a thin band of light through a mineral, like the structure of a cat's eye. Chrysoberyl, quartz and moonstone can show this property.

- **Quartz, tourmaline and hemimorphite all develop** electrical potential when subjected to mechanical stress.

- **Talc and molybdenite** are flexible and can be bent. Mica, if bent, is flexible and reverts to its original shape.

- **When a mineral has a flame directed onto it,** the colours produced are related to the mineral's chemistry. Sodium minerals colour the flame yellow, potassium gives a violet flame, and copper colours the flame green.

- **Halite, nitrate minerals and some sulphates** are soluble in water. Specimens of these have to be carefully stored.

Barite and celestite

● **Barite and celestite are both sulphates**. Barite contains the metal barium and celestite contains strontium.

● **They can both occur in hydrothermal veins** with a range of minerals, including quartz, galena, sphalerite and dolomite.

● **Barite may occur around hot springs** and in nodules in clay. Celestite can be found in evaporite deposits and hydrothermal veins.

● **As it contains barium**, barite is dense. It weighs 4.5 times as much as an equal volume of water. This helps to tell barite from other pale-coloured vein minerals.

● **Barite is usually pale-coloured** and can be white, colourless, pink, brown or grey.

● **Fine crystals of barite are common** and it also forms rounded masses called cockscomb barite.

◀ The element strontium, which occurs in celestite, is used in fireworks. Strontium gives burning fireworks a rich red colour.

● **Barite is the main ore of barium metal**. It is used in 'drilling mud', a lubricant employed when drilling for oil.

● **Celestite can be colourless**, grey, white, blue or green and often forms shiny crystals, like those of barite.

● **Celestite fluoresces under ultra-violet light**, and is slightly soluble in water.

● **Strontium is used in the manufacture of paint**, car batteries, fireworks, glass and flares.

Kyanite and garnet

▶ There are many different named types of garnet. This red-brown variety is called grossular.

● **Many minerals develop during metamorphism**. Two of the most attractive are kyanite and garnet.

● **Kyanite forms in rocks** that have been regionally metamorphosed under conditions of considerable pressure and temperature.

● **Schist and gneiss are the rocks** in which kyanite usually occurs.

● **Kyanite is often various shades of blue** but may also be pink, green, grey or yellow.

● **In schist and gneiss**, kyanite occurs as long, thin, bladed crystals.

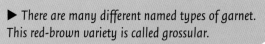
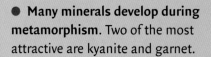
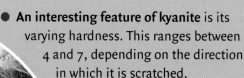

● **An interesting feature of kyanite** is its varying hardness. This ranges between 4 and 7, depending on the direction in which it is scratched.

● **Garnet is really the name** for a family of minerals. Each garnet has slightly different chemical properties.

● **Garnet commonly forms as crystals** in the cubic system. The crystals are rarely simple cubes, but more usually complex shapes with parallelogram faces.

● **Garnets can be** dark red-brown, green, orange or red.

● **As it is harder than quartz** and has attractive colours, garnet is used as a gemstone.

Malachite and azurite

● **Malachite and azurite have been prized** since the Bronze Age for their colours. The two minerals often occur together in mineral veins.

● **Both malachite and azurite are copper-bearing minerals**. They are copper carbonates.

● **Where copper veins have been altered by weathering** and contact with fluids, malachite and azurite may be found.

● **A useful test for both minerals** is applying dilute, cold hydrochloric acid to them. A chemical reaction will occur, producing bubbles of carbon dioxide.

● **Malachite is a brilliant deep green colour**, and has been used as a paint pigment for over 3000 years.

● **As it is a soft mineral** (hardness 4), malachite can be easily shaped and polished ornamentally.

● **Malachite often forms** in rounded, botryoidal masses. When cut and polished, curved patterns can appear.

● **Azurite is a rich, deep blue colour**. This mineral has also been exploited as paint pigment for thousands of years.

● **Azurite occurs in rounded masses** and also as short, stocky crystals.

● **With a hardness of only 4**, azurite can be easily scratched with a knife.

◄ *Small crystals of deep blue azurite coat this rock surface. This specimen is from the Atlas Mountains, Morocco.*

Fluorite

● **Fluorite is a common mineral** in hydrothermal veins, where it occurs with galena, calcite, quartz, borite and sphalerite.

● **Due to its chemical composition**, fluorite (calcium fluoride) has some important uses. It is used in the manufacture of hydrofluoric acid and fluorine chemicals.

● **Fluorite forms cubic and octahedral crystals**. Perfect lenses can be manufactured from fluorite crystals.

● **In the iron and steel industry**, fluorite is used as a flux. This is a material added to the molten metal to take out impurities and form the slag.

● **Fluorite is sometimes cut and facetted** as an imitation diamond.

● **In the past, fluorite was often discarded** when mineral veins were mined for lead and zinc. For this reason fine specimens can be found on old mine dumps.

◄ *These pale green, cubic crystals of fluorite are transparent, allowing light to pass through them.*

● **Fluorite is the defining mineral** at point 4 on the hardness scale.

● **An attractive banded form of fluorite**, which is found in Derbyshire, UK, is called Blue John. This is cut and polished ornamentally.

● **Fluorite is commonly purple**, green or yellowish and the crystals are transparent.

● **Often fluorite crystals interlock**. This property is called twinning. When seen in ultra-violet light, fluorite is strongly fluorescent.

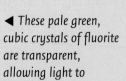

Zeolite minerals

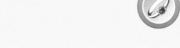

- **Zeolites usually occur** in the gas bubble hollows, called vesicles, in lavas. These hollows are left as the lava cools and gas escapes.

- **They are a group of silicate minerals** that have molecules of water in their chemical structure.

- **These minerals form when hot water** and other fluids seep through lava that has been cool for some time and buried in the Earth's crust.

- **Amygdales are the infilled gas bubble cavities** in lava. Amygdales can be made of quartz and agate as well as zeolite.

- **They have an open crystal structure**, rather like a miniature sieve. For this reason, zeolites are used to soak up moisture in industrial processes.

★ STAR FACT ★
The 'silica gel' found in small packets with cameras and electrical equipment has a zeolite structure.

- **Most zeolites are pale-coloured.** They usually form good crystals, often in a mass of thin, radiating shapes.

- **Zeolites often occur in concentric zones** in thick lava flows.

- **Stilbite is an unusual zeolite**, as the crystals are in sheaflike aggregates.

- **Zeolites are also used as water softeners**, as they are able to exchange ions. The sodium-rich zeolite called natrolite takes calcium out of hard water by exchanging its sodium for calcium.

◄ *This specimen shows fine crystals of the zeolite mineral, stilbite, growing into a cavity in basalt lava. The crystals are 1 cm long.*

Jet

- **Jet is an organic material** that is often classified with minerals.

- **The term 'jet black'** comes from this material, which is often found as layers or discrete masses in sedimentary rocks. It is therefore regarded as a sedimentary rock by many geologists.

- **Jet comes from** the Lower Jurassic strata.

- **Jet is a type of coal.** It has a high carbon content and is formed from plant material, especially the tree Araucaria, also known as the monkey puzzle tree.

- **Unlike other types of coal**, jet is found in strata deposited in the sea. Logs and other plant remains probably drifted out into the Jurassic sea, became waterlogged, sank, and were buried under sediment.

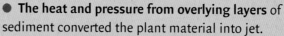

- **The heat and pressure from overlying layers** of sediment converted the plant material into jet.

- **As jet is relatively soft**, it can be easily carved. It can also be highly polished and so is used in jewellery.

- **Jet has been cut and polished** since the Bronze Age. The ancient Romans prized jewellery made from jet.

- **Queen Victoria popularized jet jewellery** in the 19th century after the death of her husband, Prince Albert. Jet was extensively mined at that time.

- **Jet has become popular again in recent years.** There are many fake items that are passed off as jet, usually made of man-made materials, including plastics.

◄ *An ancient Roman jet bangle. Jet has been cut and worked for jewellery and ornaments for over 2000 years.*

Amber

- **Amber is the fossilized resin** from ancient conifer trees, and occurs in sedimentary rocks of Cenozoic Age.

- **Amber is an organic mineral** that occurs as nodules and discrete lumps.

- **As well as the typical pale orange**, it can also be brown, greenish and black.

- **Amber is very soft** and has a splintery fracture. The surface appears resinous and transparent.

- **Much amber is found** as small 'pebbles' on beaches.

- **It is only just denser than water** and can be carried by the sea. Large amounts of amber occur in the Baltic area.

- **Amber also occurs in Romania**, Italy, France, Spain, Canada, the Dominican Republic and Russia.

- **Amber often contains small bubbles**. This is called nebulous amber.

- **Amber is very easy to carve** and for many years has been used for jewellery.

- **Fossils are often found in amber.** These are usually fossils of small insects that were stuck in fragrant resin oozing from a tree. This hardened to become amber.

◀ This fossil fly has remained unaltered since it was trapped in resin oozing from a pine tree. The resin is now amber.

Sapphire and ruby

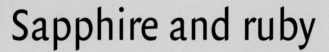

- **Corundum is aluminium oxide** and is the second-hardest mineral.

- **Usually, corundum forms** as six-sided (hexagonal) crystals with pyramids at the top and bottom.

- **Corundum can occur in many colours**, including pink, yellow, grey, green and brown. Bright-red corundum is ruby, and blue corundum is sapphire.

- **Due to its great hardness and rich colours**, corundum is much valued as a gemstone.

- **Corundum forms in igneous and metamorphic rocks**, but most of the gem quality stones are found in river shingle.

- **Famous sources of gem corundum** are Sri Lanka, Kashmir, Australia, Thailand and eastern Africa.

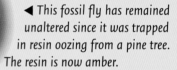

◀ These ruby crystals from India are in metamorphic rock called gneiss. The pale crystals are quartz.

- **Certain rubies are called star rubies**. These show asterism, as small needles of rutile make a star effect in the ruby.

- **Corundum is used as an abrasive.** Emery is an impure form of corundum that often also contains iron minerals.

- **Corundum can be made artificially.** August Verneuil perfected the technique as long ago as 1900.

> ★ STAR FACT ★
> Corundum crystals weighing 170 kg have been found in South Africa.

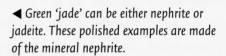

Decorative non-crystalline minerals

- **Many minerals that are non-crystalline** have great value as ornamental stones, usually due to their colours.

- **The deep blue lapis lazuli** is mainly composed of lazurite. The finest material comes from Afghanistan.

- **Lazurite contains veins of white calcite and pyrite.** It is as hard as a knife blade (hardness 5) and is translucent.

- **Turquoise is another blue**, decorative mineral, though it is generally paler than lapis lazuli.

- **Turquoise can be green** if it contains iron. Its blue colour comes from a high copper content.

◀ Green 'jade' can be either nephrite or jadeite. These polished examples are made of the mineral nephrite.

- **Much of the attractiveness of turquoise** lies in the veins of darker material that often run through it.

- **Jade is the name given to the ornamental form** of the minerals jadeite and nephrite.

- **Jadeite and nephrite** are as hard as quartz. The green variety of each is the most prized for carving.

- **Rhodonite, a complex silicate mineral**, has an attractive pink colour due to the manganese in its structure.

- **Rhodonite is used for carving** and its hardness grading of 6 makes it reasonably resistant to wear.

At home

- **A wide range of minerals and their constituents** are used in the home. These range from structural and mechanical components to food.

- **Cement, which holds the brick or stone of walls together,** is made of calcite (calcium carbonate) and mudstone. Cement is mixed with sand, which is mainly quartz.

- **Internal walls are made smooth with plaster,** which is composed largely of gypsum (calcium sulphate).

- **Electricity is carried through the house** in copper wires and water flows through copper pipes.

- **Steel, made from iron ore (hematite and magnetite),** is used for supporting lintels. It is also used to make cutlery, furniture and many other items around the home.

- **Within the home,** aluminium (from bauxite) is a common metal. It is used in cooking containers, cooking foil and washing machines.

◀ Many domestic appliances, such as washing machines, contain metals extracted from minerals.

- **Glass is manufactured from quartz sand.** It is melted and shaped into sheets or utensils. Around 2000 years ago the Romans were one of the first civilizations to make glass from quartz.

- **Salt in the kitchen** is halite (sodium chloride).

- **Cars contain aluminium** (bauxite), steel (iron ores) and copper. A car battery uses lead plates (galena) to produce an electric current.

★ STAR FACT ★
Accurate clocks and watches use very thin slices of quartz crystals to keep time.

INDEX